RISE
AND BE
HEALED

by
Father Peter McCall, OFM Cap.
and
Maryanne Lacy

HOUSE OF PEACE

BRONX, NEW YORK

Throughout this book, masculine pronouns are used as universal markers of person. This has been done in the interest of ease of reading. Please join in a loving acceptance of the limitations of our language.

Wherever real names and identities are used in this book, permission has been granted to do so. When a few have withheld their names for personal reasons, the names are fictitious, but the story is true.

Excerpts from the New American Bible © 1970 by Thomas Nelson, Publishers, Nashville and New York.

Book cover and design by Bill Murphy
Produced in the USA by Riverrun Press, Piermont, New York

ISBN: 0-936269-01-4

This book is lovingly dedicated to the beautiful Sisters of Blessed Sacrament Monastery, Yonkers, New York. They gladly provided us with space for the beginnings of the House of Peace in 1981. Their lovely Chapel has been open to us for countless Healing Masses and Services throughout the years. They have been and continue to be a source of inspiration, joy and prayerful support. Their openness, charm and friendship are priceless gifts. This ministry of healing owes much gratitude to them for the help they have given us.

We are also dedicating this book to one of our most dedicated and loyal friends Annette Giovannelli, who, coincidentally, is an alumnae of Blessed Sacrament School. Without her patience, intelligence, love and caring heart the work at the House of Peace would be overwhelming. She has taken much of the burden of the business of the House of Peace so that we can go about doing the healing work of the ministry.

This book is also dedicated to August and Therese Faustini and Julio and Francesca Mariani whose wonderful open hearts and generosity made it possible for this ministry to have a home in the Bronx, New York. We ask that God bless each and everyone of them as richly as He has blessed us with their friendship.

Table of Contents

Acknowledgements

It is with sincere and humble gratitude that we come before God in expressing our appreciation for the wonderful gift of Kathleen Garvey. Thank you, Kathleen, for coming to our rescue and transferring all our typing efforts and writings to the computer. Thank you for creating order from all the pages we sent to you. Your helpful suggestions showed a loving concern for the form and content of *Rise and Be Healed.* You are truly one of God's unconditionally loving helpers. We also thank Barbara Parrish, who worked with you. You are always in our prayers. We love you.

The Lord has surrounded us with so many gracious, loving people and so we continue to thank all the current members of The Peace of Christ Prayer Ministry for their dedication to the spread of God's healing love. We have been blessed with a loving staff at the House of Peace. Blessings upon Ursula Margagliano and Rosemarie Flick. Annette Giovanelli, our executive secretary, is truly one of the rarest of dedicated workers for the up-building of God's Kingdom here on earth. Thank you, Annette.

Our Board of Directors is a group of very wise and loving people who help direct us with their shared wisdom whenever we need assistance. We truly thank them for their love and concern.

Thank you, Father John Rathschmidt, OFM, Cap., for your most supportive letter of acknowledgement.

A most grateful thank you to Jim Scully, Pecos Benedictine, Pecos, New Mexico, for your contribution of the foreword to this book.

The cover design of this book was enhanced by the artistic talents of our good friend Bill Murphy, Santa Fe, New Mexico. Thank you, Bill, for all the time and patience in refining the pencil sketch of Jesus. We love you.

We extend gratitude to Stephen Schwartz and his wife, Donna, of Riverrun Press for their personal concern and efforts in perfecting this book and for the finishing touches to the cover.

Thank you, Steve Kormas, for the photographs of us which appear on the back cover.

We wish to extend our heartfelt and genuine thankfulness to all those dear people who responded to our cry for help for the financial support for the publication of this book. May this book bring you and all your loved ones into a greater awareness of God's total commitment to loving us all.

We wish all of God's blessings on August and Therese Faustini, Julio and Francesca Mariani and their beautiful families. They have all been the most wonderful surprises of the Holy Spirit to us. Thank you for opening up your hearts to us. Thank you for 1291 Allerton Avenue, which is home to the House of Peace.

We love you.
Father Peter McCall, OFM, Cap.
Maryanne Lacy

Office of the Provincial

30 Gedney Park Drive
White Plains, NY 10605
914-761-3008

September 24, 1991

Rev. Peter McCall, OFM Cap.
PO Box 696 1291 Allerton Avenue
Bronx, NY 10469

Dear Peter and Maryanne,

The peace of the Lord be with you!

Thank you so much for allowing me to read the advance copy of "Rise and Be Healed." As always, I find your insights and wisdom immensely helpful, especially for those who have been so hurt by the failure of our society and Church to understand or properly appreciate the devastating effect of addiction. I pray that this new work will help thousands of people to be unafraid of their illness. As you so clearly say throughout your book, illness faced is the first step in getting to know God in a totally different way.

Congratulations! Your book is a good one and a fine contribution to the growing literature of spirituality in the light of the Twelve Steps of AA.

With every good wish and prayer, I am yours

In Christ,
Father Jack Rathschmidt, OFM Cap.
Provincial Minister
Capuchin Franciscans

Foreword

Health is much on the minds of Americans these days. The main reason for our concern is financial. We are finding it harder and harder to pay for medical insurance. In fact, millions of people cannot afford any kind of insurance. Millions more find their insurance costs climbing so high that their budgets are being stretched to the bursting point — and these are people from the middle class, not the poor.

Medical costs, rising at more than twice the inflation rate, threaten the very profitability of major corporations. As government officials scour the world to uncover a more inclusive, less expensive way to structure our medical care, perhaps each citizen should join them in taking a fresh and wide-sweeping look at the whole question of healing. Perhaps we should even dare to ask the question, "Why do we get sick in the first place?"

One simple way to do that would be to read this book. Simple, but not entirely soothing. Father McCall and Maryanne have a prophetic streak in them. They challenge us to get involved in our healing, not to wait passively for an instant cure from outside ourselves. We tend to view sickness as an interruption in our regular routine; we want somebody — doctor, healer or mom — to get rid of it for us. The authors, however, do not consider sickness a marginal nuisance; they locate health at the very heart of life itself. They see sickness and healing as largely an outflow of things inside of us — attitudes, decisions, beliefs.

This can be disturbing news. We may recoil from such an outlook. We may not want to accept any responsibility for our health or lack of it. But then we are part of the problem that businessmen and politicians strain to resolve. We are sitting on the beach watching the wave of the future roll on without us. For to an increasing degree the world is coming to realize that many aspects of our health are in our own hands. Just think of how the tide has turned against smoking, how we count calories and cholesterol, how we are becoming a nation of exercisers.

Rise and Be Healed is the right kind of upsetting news: the kind that turns out to be good news. As the health care crisis grows ever more severe, it sounds the alarm that something is terribly amiss. The old is no longer working and may not be workable. We need something new.

Father McCall and Maryanne Lacy offer us a radically different vision. They dare to tell the truth as they have discovered it. They ask us to widen our concept of health to embrace far more than drugs and surgery, important as these are. They champion the spiritual dimension of healing, all but lost in our materialistic culture. Drawing from their many years of experience as ministers of God's healing, they point out realities that we may be unaware of, realities that may exert a powerful influence on the shape of our lives and on the state of our health.

Rise and Be Healed is thus an important book that comes at the right time. Its message is the one we need to hear at this moment. Its challenge offers us the opportunity to look in new directions, see with clearer vision and open ourselves to the ways in which the Spirit of God is moving in the 1990's.

I do not think it is possible to read *Rise and Be Healed* and not be changed for the better.

Jim Scully

A Journey To Wholeness

December 6, 1988
Dear Father Peter and Maryanne,

This is a long, long overdue thank you letter. I have been wanting to tell you how much you and the Peace of Christ Prayer Ministry have helped me. Your First Saturday Masses have played a vital role in my life these past few years. I began attending the Masses in 1982. Since then I have only missed a couple Masses when I was traveling; otherwise I use this day each month to revitalize myself spiritually.

During these past six years, my life has changed so dramatically that they seem as one year; one long continuous year of changes, healings, growing, maturing and renewing. And I am certain that all these changes have been guided by the Spirit of God through both of you and the members of your prayer ministry who are also so gifted. When I became involved in the Charismatic Renewal in 1976, like so many of us after our Baptism in the Spirit, I experienced the renewed joy of God's love for me and with this experience the insatiable desire for more. I had been attending my regular prayer meeting, and all of the conferences being held in the Northeast, plus many, many workshops on inner healing. We do not have a regularly scheduled Healing Mass in Manhattan, therefore, when I heard of your First Saturday Masses, I began the trek to Yonkers each month.

I am convinced that it was at your Healing Masses that all those prayers for healing finally came to fruition; month after month of the Liturgy, praise, teaching, and the peaceful prayer, slowly peeled away all sorts of hurts, angers, resentments and deep-seated fears. Things in my psyche that I was never even aware existed, but things that prevented me from being a whole, healthy person, were prayed away without the least bit of pain.

I began to let go of my own ideas of security and to seek those things that gave me the peace, trust, love and truth that can only come from the Holy Spirit. I found this and much, much more. Of course, there is no doubt in my mind that in addition to all the inner healing I've received, all your prayers for physical healing have helped me too. As you are always saying: "God is good."

God knows what we need. In fact, after having been prayed over at each Mass for several years, I stopped asking for individual prayer, because I realized that it was as you sang in tongues, Maryanne, at the healing portion of the day that I received the healing. Often two or three days passed and then something would surface, usually in prayer, that told me some area of my life had been touched by Jesus and a healing had occurred. God is good. During these years, I brought many people to the Blessed Sacrament Chapel with me, some of whom still attend regularly. Everyone has thanked me profusely for introducing them to your Mass. Some remarkable healings and stories have occurred. Each one has remarked after the first visit to the Chapel that he/she has never experienced so much love in any prayer group. I agree. The Blessed Sacrament Chapel is truly Holy Ground; the music is always a joy; and the hospitality is a healing experience all its own.

I must also mention that your book, "An Invitation to Healing", and your tapes, have also been a real source of healing. Each person I have shared them with cherishes them, especially those in need of sustained soaking prayer.

Lastly, but far from the least, I want to say "Amen" to all the wonderful teachings I have heard over these years. Your homilies, Father Peter, are certainly an integral part of healing. Such good, sound teaching can only lead to good, sound thinking — the first step to transformation. Again, I share your homilies as well as the printed meditations you publish.

Over the years, the wonderful experiences through your Masses have been innumerable; there is no way to really thank both of you and your prayer group for all the prayers, patience and, especially all your hard work — I know the ministry you were called to is unquestionably the most exhausting. My friends and I pray for you all the time as our way of saying thank you to the Lord for your ministry.

Sincerely,
Kathleen Garvey
New York, NY

Preface

Where We Left Off. . .

God is always full of surprises! When our book, *An Invitation to Healing*, was written in 1985, we were still at our old center in Yonkers, NY. After the book was published, our ministry grew at such a rapid rate that our center, known as the House of Peace, became far too small for us. So, sometime in 1986 I contacted a friend of mine who sells real estate and asked her to be on the lookout for some property or a building for us so that we could expand. About the same time, without knowing we were seeking more space, a friend of ours called and said that a woman in the Bronx, NY wanted to use a building she owned for God's purposes and had us in mind. After some weeks we finally met this mysterious woman. Her name is Theresa Faustini and she was not so mysterious at all. A few years earlier she had visited the House of Peace with her mother who was going through a depression. After prayer, her mother recovered. This good woman asked us if we were interested in a proposal. Her husband, August, and her father, Julio Mariani, were in the building and contracting business. They had just acquired a building which they had built in 1952; the building had been abandoned by the previous owners and had fallen into shambles. Theresa, being a prayerful woman, asked for guidance. She wanted the building to be used for some combination of medical health care and healing prayer. As she placed this dream before the Lord, she saw an image of Father Peter in her mind. She felt that God was directing her and her family to invite our ministry to use the building in conjunction with other health care professionals who believed in the healing power of Jesus Christ. Soon after this meeting, we set a date to see the building. It was hard to imagine at the time what could be done with the building because it was in such bad shape. With the talents of August Faustini and his construction company, who worked hard at restoring it, the building was completely gutted and revamped to provide everyone with clean and efficient space. It was finally completed in March 1988.

With the help of our good friends, we made the move from Yonkers, NY to 1291 Allerton Avenue in the East Bronx, NY. We have lovely modern offices and a prayer room. People from our ministry chipped in and donated desks, furniture, and decorations. Jane Byrne and her daughter, Isabel Milano, contributed their organizational skills. The powers of heaven were at work seeing to it that we were made quite comfortable to do our work.

We continue to have our First Saturday of the Month Healing Mass at Blessed Sacrament Monastery Chapel in Yonkers, NY, together with a Tuesday noon healing service. We are happy to have the prayer support of the loving Sacramentine Sisters who live and pray there. We also want to mention our friend, confidante, and loyal worker, Annette Giovannelli, who sees to it that everything in the House of Peace runs smoothly.

We want to thank Theresa and August Faustini and their family for allowing God to use them so that we could continue to bring God's comfort and compassion to those who seek it. We want to thank the Sacramentine Sisters for all these years of support and love. Also, thank you, Annette, for all you do for us. Now you know why we dedicated this book to these people.

Other Changes as Well

Changes usually come about through pain and it was through a personal experience of pain that we entered into a new phase of our ministry. The problem began about the same time the ministry was accelerating rapidly. More and more people were responding to the call of healing in their lives. I was not quite sure how to handle so many pressing requests. I was going through a period of burnout which can be quite common in the healing prayer ministry; I was trying to please everyone and at the same time feeling exhausted. There was a particular group of people whom I considered to be putting a disproportionate amount of expectations on Father Peter and me. They felt that our time with them should be given top priority. They were putting demands on us which I believed to be unreasonable. It seemed to me that they were trying to make us feel guilty. My confusion and hurt was compounded when one of them told me that there was talk going around against us. I felt betrayed. My conscience told me that Father Peter and I had done the best we could under the circumstances. I knew we had acted with the best intentions, but they were not enough to satisfy.

My emotional anguish continued for some months. One evening I shared my pain with a friend who was a counselor with our ministry, Tina Jablonowski. She asked me if I had ever heard of "co-dependency." I told her that I had never even heard the word. A few days later she dropped off a book at my home. This book was to change my life and the direction of our ministry. The name of the book is *Co-Dependency: Misunderstood, Mistreated* (Harper & Row, 1986) by Ann Wilson Schaef. God bless Tina for caring and introducing me to the concept of co-dependence. God knew what I needed to learn at that time and I was prepared to learn it. Thank you, Tina, for listening to the Holy Spirit's guidance.

The walls of denial came tumbling down as I read about the symptoms of co-dependency. Among the characteristics I could identify with easily were not trusting one's own perceptions, being a martyr, caretaking, and perfectionism. I had been trying to please too many people at my own expense in order to be accepted and loved. Being a martyr and being gullible were at the top of the list. The author also pointed out that co-dependents were notoriously poor judges of character. I was relieved, to say the least, to realize that I was not alone and that there was help.

I shared the book and my insights about it with Father Peter; he was obviously curious and interested. We were soon to learn that there were many books written on the subject of co-dependency. We learned about the Adult Children of Alcoholics, dysfunctional family systems, and how they are all interconnected with one another. We learned about the family roles that children have to play in order to survive in a dysfunctional family: the family hero, the lost child, the scapegoat, and the mascot of the family.

Soon after our arrival in the Bronx, I received a flyer in the mail advertising the book, *Bradshaw on the Family* (Health Communications, 1988). I felt that stirring of excitement familiar to me when I'm following the direction of the Holy Spirit. I ordered the book. Within a matter of a few days someone else gave the book to Father Peter. We knew we were on to something. I decided to send for the video cassette tapes of John Bradshaw after reading the book. He is a dynamic speaker, and his subject was healing the dysfunctional family.

Our ministry has long been concerned with healing the root causes of disease and preventing sickness through teaching and healing prayer. We realized that the problem of co-dependency was deeply rooted in the dysfunctional family system, which our addicted society propagates. We began to understand how the disease of co-dependency, if left untreated, can be life-threatening. Most active alcoholics tend to outlive their co-dependent spouses. Co-dependents tend to develop gastro-intestinal disorders, migraine headaches, difficulty in breathing, and heart problems. Even cancer has been associated with co-dependency. Practically every adult child of an alcoholic that I have prayed with has had stomach problems to one degree or another.

The material that John Bradshaw presented both fascinated and shocked me. His openness on subjects such as child abuse, incest, sexual and physical abuse was unfamiliar to my Irish puritanical background. My walls of denial were crumbling. I come from a physically and emotionally abusive family. This had been no secret to me, but the defenses that I had placed in my mind were definitely co-dependent. I knew that I still needed a great deal of healing myself.

According to John Bradshaw, the symptoms of sick thinking that are present in families of adult children of alcoholics are also present in families that have histories of mental depression, hypochondria, overeating disorders, sexual and physical abuse, etc. Dysfunctional family systems have permeated society in general—ninety-six percent of our families are dysfunctional according to statistics. Father Peter and I embarked on a commitment to learn all there was to learn on this subject in order to help ourselves and those with whom we have been called to pray. Out of our pain came a new light. We began to understand what had happened to us. Through the reading material that was presented to us on the question of co-dependency, we saw how important the twelve step programs are to healing.

There is a twelve step support group for almost every human problem. I decided to join a co-dependent's group in order to understand the subject better. In attending, I realized how much healing I really needed. Our ministry began to take on a completely new dimension.

In our first book, *An Invitation to Healing*, we shared how God led us to a greater understanding of the healing of cancer and other life-threatening diseases. Little did we know at that time that we would be led to more knowledge through understanding dysfunctional family systems. "God works through mysterious ways, His wonders to perform." Father Peter is the teacher in this ministry. He believes that his mission is to teach as Jesus taught. We know that healing is taking place when issues are being raised and when people recognize what is wrong with them and then put a name on it. Father Peter calls it "healing by explanation." Often we hear people say, "Now I know what is wrong. Now I can work on it." They have a sense of relief because they are not alone.

I believe now more than ever that God intends His people to live in health, happiness, and prosperity. In learning our lessons of love and forgiveness with the Holy Spirit, we can turn adversity into victory. I know this is true from my own experience. In the early part of 1982, I went through a separation in my marriage of twenty-five years. During the following years, I could have chosen to despair many times, but my faith was always my guide and friend. The separation finally ended in divorce in 1989. Jesus promised us his peace, the peace that passes all understanding.

We believe that all things are possible because we are followers of Jesus Christ. He tells us in John's gospel, "Until now you have not asked for anything in my name. Ask and you shall receive that your joy may be full" (16:24). To quote Emily Dickinson, "So, instead of getting to Heaven at last . . . I'm going all along." Father Peter and I desire that this book will reach you and touch you so that you will Rise And Be Healed in the name of Jesus Christ!

God bless you.

I love you.
Maryanne Lacy

RISE

AND BE

HEALED

Chapter 1

RISE AND BE HEALED OF THE ROOT OF DISEASE

> *"For I will restore you to health; of your wounds I will heal you, says the Lord"* *(Jeremiah 30:17A).*

Since we wrote *An Invitation to Healing* in 1985 much has happened to make us want to write this new book. We have been saying since the beginning of our ministry over ten years ago that it was never enough just to pray for the removal of symptoms of a sickness. There is so much more to sickness than meets the eye. We said in our first book that Jesus wants to heal causes, not effects. He wants to heal roots, not symptoms. We knew very early in our ministry that we had to take a holistic approach to healing. We knew that prayer alone was not enough. We were very much aware that authentic healing included change in lifestyle, proper diet, stress reduction, and change in attitudes. Prayer and meditation are part of a program for health, but not the whole story.

1

Since we wrote our first book, we have gotten involved with the work of the Adult Children of Alcoholics and the spirituality of the Twelve Step Program. From this movement, which we firmly believe was inspired by the Holy Spirit, we have received greater insight into the root causes of sickness and disease. In fact, I would call it more a "breakthrough" than an insight because it revolutionized our approach to disease by revealing the spiritual root of all sickness.

The literature of the ACOA and similar twelve step programs have pointed out the destructive effects that a dysfunctional family has on the lives of many people. A dysfunctional family is any family in which there is irrational, violent, abusive, addictive, or repressive behavior, or which is dominated by an addictive or neurotic personality. It has been estimated that ninety-six percent of the families in the United States fall into this category to some extent. The degree of dysfunctionality will obviously vary between families, but the sad fact is that millions of people have been negatively affected by addictive and abusive behavior within the family.

We will talk in greater detail throughout this book about some specific dysfunctions within families and how they promote sickness and disease. We maintain in this book that it is the dysfunctional family itself which is the breeding ground for the seeds which eventually become the roots of sickness and disease.

What all dysfunctional families have in common is that they are "shame based." This means that not only is shame used to manipulate and control its members, but the addictive and abusive behavior within the family actually "shames" its members. Any child who was abused physically, emotionally, or sexually has been "shamed." Every family in which there is addictive or compulsive behavior, whether it be with alcohol, food, drugs, sex, work, or religion, "shames" its members.

We will talk more specifically about shame and guilt in chapter three of this book. We want to point out here that shame is the "tap root" from which many sicknesses and diseases originate. Shame is a spiritual problem and therefore only a spiritual program can bring healing.

The Twelve Step Program was originally intended to help the alcoholic. It recognizes that alcoholism is a spiritual problem that only a Higher Power can heal. The psychiatrist, Carl Jung, told Bill W., the co-founder of Alcoholics Anonymous, that only a spiritual experience would heal him of his addiction. On the night of December 13, 1934, in Towns Hospital, New York City, Bill W. had a spiritual experience and for the next thirty-six years he did not take a drink. He went on to co-found Alcoholics Anonymous which has spread around the world and helped countless millions of people to achieve serenity and healing.

We are discovering in our day that the spiritual truths expressed in the Twelve Step Program not only can help alcoholics, but also can help anyone who comes from a dysfunctional family within our addicted society. I foresee the day when even cancer will be healed in the format of an AA meeting, by a group of loving and non-judgmental people sitting around sharing their deepest feelings and experiences and following the direction of the Inner Guide, the Holy Spirit or Higher Power. I now believe that all healing, physical or psychological, in some way, must be spiritual healing. Alcoholics Anonymous has an expression, "There is no chemical solution to a spiritual problem." I will go so far as to say that all forms of sickness and disease are spiritual problems and need a spiritual program for healing.

Shame, which I consider as the root of all our problems, is a spiritual problem because it is based on the misconception that our very being is defective. Shame implies something about the Creator of our being. If we believe something is radically wrong with us, then we are saying that God did something wrong to us. This is a spiritual problem and must be dealt with at that level.

What I would like to do in this first chapter is share with you what I consider the healing wisdom in the twelve step spirituality and how I feel it gets to the root of our problems. I call these principles the Twelve Healing Truths. They form the foundation on which the rest of the material in this book is based. They represent much of the information and insight we have gained in these past five years.

The Twelve Healing Truths

1. Healing is Dying to Our False-Self. This first truth contains the whole healing process in a nutshell. Healing begins where our own personal resources end. Only when we reach the realization of personal powerlessness can a Higher Power take over. This is basically the first step of the Twelve Step Program. We have to reach our personal "bottom" before we will call out for help. We must reach a "teachable moment" when we are open to new options because the old options aren't working. All defenses, such as denial and projection, no longer serve us and the pain has become so bad that we are willing to do anything that will help.

In traditional spirituality, this is the moment of metanoia, the moment of conversion, when we decide that the direction in which we have been going is getting us nowhere and we decide to "turn around." It is described in Jesus' parable of the Prodigal Son as the moment when "he came to his senses" (Lk 15:17). Unless this moment is reached, I do not believe that authentic healing can take place because we leave room for the bargaining and rationalizations which keep us from our healing. We must be willing to challenge everything we have believed up to the present moment and come to our healing with an open mind.

2. Healing is Faith in a Power Beyond Us, but is Within Us. In a moment of grace (a spiritual awakening) we become aware of a Power that is within us and available to us that will help us in restoring sanity and health. A deep spiritual experience is not needed at this point, but simply an awareness that we are not alone in our journey toward health and that there is a spiritual power who is helping us and guiding us. This "Power" is benign and non-judgmental. It is a helping force which empowers us to do what we could never do on our own.

In order to accept this Higher Power, we must be willing to question any belief we have in a God of wrath and condemnation. One of the reasons why many churches have failed to heal is because they maintain guilt and shame by teaching separation and elitism. These are the very beliefs that inhibit healing because they do not reveal God as a consistent helper and healer. We will never go to a God for healing who at the same time might afflict us. The reason that Alcoholics Anonymous has been successful where the churches have failed is because it is a non-sectarian movement which neither advocates nor supports any particular form of religion. However, it is a spiritual program and does emphasize the need for a spiritual power beyond ourselves as a means for attaining healing. To have faith in a Higher Power which helps and guides us, we must be willing to put aside many of our notions about God and simply have faith that a Power beyond our own is willing to help and heal us.

3. Healing is Accepting Our Good as Gift. One of the hidden heresies of our day is that we have to earn our salvation and healing. Yet, people who have been healed of a serious disease will tell you they did nothing to deserve to be healed, but that they simply cooperated with grace. Many people ask, "What must I do to be healed?" But, what they really mean is, "What cost must I pay?" or, "What must I sacrifice?" We all have a deep investment in the "merit system," and until we realize that healing is a gift that must be accepted, we will remain in a state of bargaining and manipulating to get our healing.

We have to learn how to accept God's freely given gifts without the guilt of thinking that we have to pay God back. We have always been taught that if people give us gifts, we automatically have an obligation to give something in return. This makes many hesitant to accept healing because they fear what might be expected of them in return. Such an attitude degrades God and brings God down to our level. God is beyond our human images. Saint Paul realized this when he wrote, "It's all grace" (Rom 4:16).

4. Healing is Faith in Action. Once we have acknowledged personal powerlessness and come to the realization that only a Power beyond our own can heal us, we must turn our will and life over to this Higher Power by listening and obeying. This is the third Step of the Twelve Step Program.

Someone once wrote, "Let no one be deluded that knowledge of the path can substitute for putting one foot in front of the other." This is the other side of the coin of faith. On one side we have Paul telling us that "It's all grace" (Rom 4:16), and on the other side we have St. James telling us, "Faith without works is dead" (James 2:26). These statements do not contradict one another; they go together. Once you accept the free gift of healing from God, you express that acceptance by acting on it. This is evidenced in many of the miracles of Jesus where he asked the person who wanted to be healed to do something; "Stretch forth your hand!" (Mk 3:5); "Take up your mat!" (Jn 5:8). What he is saying is that we are to step out in faith. Healing is a gift, but we accept it by acting on it.

Alcoholics Anonymous has a powerful saying, "Fake it till you make it." This phrase is not asking us to be deceitful, instead it's telling us that we have to practice our healing. We must actively participate in the gift so that it can take root in us, otherwise, we fall into the heresy of "quietism." We should not remain totally passive to the gifts of God. We are "co-creators" with God in our healing.

5. Healing is Accepting Personal Responsibility. Our experience has been that "healing begins where blaming leaves off." We cannot afford the luxury of seeing ourselves as victims of the world around us. The acceptance of victims is related to a false perception of martyrdom. The martyrs were praised and canonized in the early church because they would rather face a horrible death than deny their faith in Jesus. Where the misperception developed was that the suffering of these martyrs (the word means witness) was glorified rather than their free choice to die instead of denying Jesus. These witnesses were not passive victims, but active participants in testifying to their faith in Jesus by dying rather than denying their faith. Somewhere along the line, the word "martyr" came to mean someone who passively submits to suffering. This is simply not true.

The martyrs of the early Church were not victims nor was Jesus. In John's Gospel it is apparent that Jesus was in complete control of what was occurring during the last days of his life. He says, "This is why the Father loves me, because I lay down my life in order to take it up again. *No one takes it from me, but I lay it down on my own.* I have the power to lay it down, and the power to take it up again" (Jn 10:17-8). It is clear in John's theology that Jesus was not a victim and we are not to view Jesus as an example of passive submission to suffering.

AlAnon has an expression, "We may have been victims as children, but as adults we're volunteers." If we want to be healed, we have to let go of the idea that healing and peace depend on someone else changing. Authentic change can only take place in our minds. Healing can't happen anywhere else.

6. Healing is Non-rational. We do not have to fully understand what we are doing before we do it. There's an old expression, "Analysis leads to paralysis." One of the greatest obstacles to healing is rationalization because trying to figure everything out before we do anything leads to procrastination. We are actually resisting healing when we insist that we must have all the answers before we take a step toward healing.

Healing is non-rational because it is not the result of left brain reasoning, but rather right brain insight and intuition. We will never be able to reason ourselves into a healing. We try to do this because we want to be in charge of the healing and in control of the whole process. To depend on our right brain with its imagination and creativity is too risky for people who need to be in control. Some people are afraid to take the risk that healing implies. Our experience in the healing ministry is that intellectual people are the most difficult to heal.

Healing is non-rational, not irrational. Just because we do not know how healing works does not mean that there are not spiritual laws which bring it about. We do not have to know a lot about disease to be healed. All we need to know is what it takes to get well. We will be told what it takes by our Higher Power who speaks to us through the creative and imaginative part of our mind.

7. Healing is Commitment to Life. Our experience in a healing prayer ministry has shown us that one characteristic seems to dominate in those who were healed — "an urge toward life". This commitment toward life has nothing to do with the fear of death. It is true that some people stay alive because they fear death, but fear does not heal. It merely prolongs the misery. What contributes to healing is "a joy of living," a life-urge which overcomes any death wish no matter how subtle it may be.

Someone once said, "The question is not, 'Is there life after death, but, is there life before death?'" Healing is choosing those options which promote and encourage life. This is seen most clearly in people who take a "holistic" approach to living and express life in various ways. These people are not bored nor do they lead "lives of quiet desperation." They see life as good and therefore enjoy it. There is an Irish blessing which says, "May you live until you die." Those people who make a commitment to life personify this blessing. They seem to heal more quickly than others because they want to get on with living.

8. Healing is Forgiveness. All healing involves some form of forgiveness. I would go so far as to say that healing is synonymous with forgiveness. We cannot have one without the other. Forgiveness has been the secret law of healing for too long. I do not

10

understand why people wait for deathbed scenes before they will forgive. Forgiveness is so powerful in the healing process that we should not wait until we are sick to do it.

The message of the healing power of forgiveness has been at the heart of our ministry since we began. The one chapter in our first book, *An Invitation to Healing,* which had the most favorable response was on forgiveness. Basically, forgiveness is the willingness to let go of all forms of attack toward someone else because we know that we can never experience healing while the poisons of bitterness and resentment remain in our bodies. If sickness and disease are forms of attack upon our body then it is only in giving up our belief that attack gets us what we want that we can be healed.

9. Healing is Re-pairation. Healing is correction without punishment. Notice that this principle says "re-pairation" and not reparation. Reparation, in the sense of atonement, has taken on a meaning that connotes some form of punishment. Punishment has nothing to do with repairing any harm done. Only in a sick world do people believe that the suffering of another makes up for harm done. Only healing has the power to restore what has been lost.

True re-pairation does not bring pain or suffering, but correction on the level that the harm was done. Re-pairation is a part of justice, but justice and love are the same virtue. Re-pairation is simply completing unfinished business — doing or saying something today which should have been done or said in the past. Making amends means to mend, to heal a wound or hurt by a present act of love.

Making amends is healing because it brings closure to our relationships. We do today what we should have done in the past and we do it in a loving way. Making amends should not create more problems or be done in the manner of attack or anger. The Higher Power knows the importance of re-pairation and will direct and guide us in the exact manner that it should be done.

10. Healing is Process. Healing is not magic. It took time to get sick, so it will take time to get well. Just as we were conditioned toward disease, we have to be re-educated toward wholeness. The de-programming must be done without skipping steps. We know from psychology that defenses should not be taken away too quickly or we will panic and feel vulnerable. So it is with healing. We can be healed only to the extent that we are ready to accept a new way of life. Healing is always a change and change can be frightening. Healing is a journey which we take at a pace that does not cause fear.

11. Healing is Perseverance. Alcoholics Anonymous has an expression, "It's not perfection but persistence we want." Healing is not a perfect process. It can, in fact, get rather sloppy. We can fall quite often in our journey toward wholeness. We must be persistent in turning our "setbacks into comebacks."

Our experience in the healing prayer ministry has shown us that it is the people who consistently come back to our healing services that experience healing. They are like the woman in Jesus' parable of the persistent widow (Lk 18:1-18) or the story of the man who goes to his friend's house at night seeking bread (Lk 11:5-8). They get what they need because they did not get discouraged, but "seek, knock, and ask" with perseverance.

Perseverance in prayer is not overcoming God's unwillingness to give, but sets us up to receive. It's equivalent to "stepping out in faith." At some level, we would not persevere in prayer unless we were convinced that we already have received what we are asking for.

I have had people say to me, "I was at your healing service last week, but I wasn't healed." With that one flippant remark, off they go with the conviction that no one is healed at our services, or that God does not want them healed. Actually, both of these assumptions are wrong, but these people will never know because they did not persevere.

12. Healing is Sharing What We Have Received. In the program of Alcoholic Anonymous, this principle is called "Twelve Stepping." It is actually done for a very selfish motive. If we do not reach out and share with others what we have received, we will lose it. We share what we have received, not to manipulate or control others, but to maintain our own health, serenity, and sanity.

Someone once said, "Love is not love until you give it away." It is only love that heals and it is love that maintains our healing. If we hope to be healed, we must be willing to share our healing with others.

The success of the twelve step programs can be found in those people who were healed through the programs and who continue to reach out to others. It is not an accident that you can phone an Alcoholics Anonymous office at any time, day or night, and

13

get a friendly answer. These people are there because they have discovered the principle that Jesus taught long ago - giving and receiving are the same (Lk 6:37, 38). We are healed as we heal.

These Twelve Healing Truths will appear throughout the rest of this book. We will apply them to specific problems created by the dysfunctional family in our society. They go to the root cause of many of our problems. As with the twelve steps themselves, there is nothing radically new here. They are principles which have been proven by time and have worked before and will work again. I pray that they be helpful to you.

Father Peter McCall

Reflections and Sharing

RISE AND BE HEALED OF THE ROOT OF DISEASE

Father Peter refers to me as the "Responsorial Psalm". In all our workshops and retreats I try to respond to his teaching. It is a tough act to follow. Father Peter is perhaps one of the finest teachers on the scene today. He is a man who struggles with stuttering. God uses him despite it. He is quite courageous. I know he wouldn't like me to spread it around, but he is a humble man. Humble in the sense that he must rely on the power of Holy Spirit to work through him. I believe it takes a lot of courage to be healed and Father Peter has shown that courage every time he steps out in faith and speaks from the podium. Recently, a young man passed me a note after listening to us giving talks on a retreat. The note read, "I feel glad... encouraged...re: teachings of today and the power and peace that I've found possible by becoming more personally aware of

Jesus and that my credibility doesn't come from my peers, but from within."

It takes a great deal of courage to be healed because fear of the unknown and fear of change so often get in the way. When we "get sick of being sick," we will either make a decision to be healed or make a decision to die.

I have been on this journey of healing prayer now for almost twenty years. I mentioned in our book, An Invitation to Healing, *about my struggle with depression and my victory over it. I recall during that period reading a book by the Linn Brothers about the healing of memories. They challenged the reader to take a risk in order to be healed. I figured at the time that I had little to lose, so after Mass one morning, I made a conscious decision to risk being healed. I was sick of being sick and I wanted to be free from fears, violence, and unhappiness. I have never regretted that decision. People who know me now would never be able to recognize the person I used to be. The fact is, neither do I. It all seems like a bad dream and a bad trip. I have never been happier or healthier than I am right now. Following Jesus and being true to His call for me has produced abundant fruit. His call to us is, "Come, follow me," and His promise is Peace.*

The theme of this first chapter is "Rise and Be Healed From the Root Causes of Sickness." This root begins to develop early in our childhood when we strive to live up to the expectations of those in authority over us. It begins when we start to not-be-true to ourselves. It is absolutely necessary to have a spiritual awakening and to be committed to a spiritual life. When we do, we will find that Heaven is at our beck and call giving us guidance along the way. We were created in the image and likeness of God (Genesis 1:27). We are being called out of darkness into the Light (Acts 27:17).

Not too long ago, a friend gave me a great compliment. He said, "Maryanne, you are not just a survivor, you are a thriver." I was pleased with that comment because I believe we are all meant to thrive and not just survive. It saddens me that so many people are barely surviving, let alone thriving. For so many who come to our services life is one struggle upon another. We have a Higher Power. It is the Power of the Holy Spirit. He is our support system, and so there is no need to simply struggle along.

One of the characteristics of co-dependency is dishonesty. It is intrinsically dishonest to live the life that other people expect us to live. We are meant to restore our true identity. In our first book, we wrote about the "counterfeit self" and the "authentic self." If we are not true to ourselves and live lives of quiet desperation (sometimes not so quiet,) our bodies, minds and emotions will send us the bill.

For years, I had stomach problems, migraine headaches, neuralgia, disorders and depression. I come from a severely abusive and violent family system. People who come from this type of background suffer from many of these symptoms and more. Depending upon the severity of the abuse and the form of abuse, the symptoms of physical and emotional problems can be enormous. Yet, many do not put two and two together;

*they do not realize that the symptoms are the effect and
not the cause.*

*I will be forever grateful for the many forms of
healing that have helped me back to health and in
maintaining it. I have used various therapists, counseling, laying on of hands, nutrition, exercise, herbal
remedies, vitamins and tender loving care. I have become aware that I need to be self-caring in order to
remain healthy.*

*As I look back on my years in the healing ministry,
even though I have given of myself to the healing of
others, I too was a recipient. I think that in God's plan
everything that we give to others will be returned to us
(Lk6:37,38). Of course, that can work both negatively
and positively; therefore, we need to beware of what we
are sowing.*

*Co-dependents are notorious for helping others to
the detriment of their own well-being. I had to learn by
trial and error to balance my work in the healing prayer
ministry and how to take care of myself. Balance and
harmony are keynote words, otherwise we may open
ourselves up to a weak immune system and be prone to
sickness.*

*I was delightfully surprised a few years ago when
I was given a gentle reminder through the writings of
St. Vincent De Paul (1581-1660). A friend passed this
quote on to me and it read:*

Take great care to preserve your health for the
love of Our Lord and His poor members, and
beware of doing too much. It is one of the evil
one's tricks to deceive good souls into doing

more than they are able to do, until they are capable of nothing at all. But the Spirit of God gently bids them to do what good they reasonably can, so that they persevere in doing good for a long time.

What makes this statement so impressive is that it comes from a time in church history when the heresy of Jansenism was widespread and sacrifice and suffering were considered saintly virtues. The body was considered evil. It encouraged me to see that the Catholic Church had canonized someone with good common sense.

As part of my self-caring program I am aware that I must be vigilant over my thoughts and attitudes. On page 167 of An Invitation to Healing, *I shared my story of the threat of breast cancer, since then I have been keenly conscious of the need for continuous healing of root causes, lest the tumor develop again. For those of us who have a tendency toward self-destruction, this vigilance is a lifetime process, it requires discipline. It requires a lot of letting go. By this I mean, what are my priorities? As Father Peter points out quite often, would I rather be right or happy?*

I have made a commitment to myself to practice a holistic way of life in order to maintain health. I believe that if more of us practiced preventive health care, there would be less sickness. I don't mean just taking care of the body, but developing healthy attitudes and a healthy spiritual life.

Many people confuse healing with magic. They want someone or something to make everything all better instantly. Making a commitment to themselves seems to be too big for many people to handle, yet, there is no way around it. Healing is participating with the Holy Spirit. The choice is always there. I believe that we get sick for many reasons but essentially it is a defense against God's love. However, illness can become a great opportunity to bring us close to God as we seek His Love in healing us. In healing the root cause of sickness, we must allow the barriers of fear, especially the fear of God's love, to be removed.

New Life

I am most delighted to report that every person whose testimony of healing we placed in our book, An Invitation to Healing, *is still maintaining his or her health. Praise God from whom all blessings flow! We have lost touch with some of the people, but most of them keep in touch with us. Jane Clark, whose profound testimony on page 127, is absolutely a new creation. She has given birth to her third child this past summer. Jane now has three boys, all delivered by Caesarean section. In spite of various stresses, such as a miscarriage and a change of job for her husband, she is still healthy and free from all symptoms of multiple sclerosis. Jane has an aura of inner peace about her and she has been given a new inner strength that will see her through life's knockabouts. Thank you, Jesus!*

Carl Saueracker, page 177, reported a healing from Chronic Lymphocytic Leukemia in 1983. Carl practices preventive medicine by continuing to receive healing prayer. Recently, he and his wife, Nancy, took an extensive and vigorous tour of Eastern Europe. He has retired and is planning more trips. God bless you, Carl!

Baby Louis, page 158, is no longer a baby. Louis is now eight years old. When he was just six months old, he was diagnosed as having a rare bone marrow disease known as myelo fibrosis and through healing prayer was completely cured. He came with his mother, Maria, to visit us at the House of Peace in the Bronx. He is cute, funny and loves to make his mother laugh. During their visit, we prayed with Maria, who was going through some family stress—she has five children. (After Louis, she had a girl Tara, who is five years old.) As we prayed with Maria, Louis was by her side; Father Peter anointed her with oil and asked God to give her the courage to deal with all the stresses in her life. It was all very solemn. When Father Peter finished, eight year old Louis said to him, "Father, when you were praying, I bet my mother was thinking: 'Hey, God, will you help me lose fifty pounds?'" His mother burst out laughing and said, "I swear, that's just what I was thinking, but I didn't want to say it because I didn't want to sound selfish."

The story of Hilda, on page 96, is a wonderful inspiration. She has had no recurrence of cancer since we wrote about her in 1985. Hilda is quite committed to her wellness, always seeking ways in which she can grow and learn. She is vigilant over her attitudes and maintains her health through holistic approaches. She, too, is living an active spiritual life. Life has taken on a whole new meaning for her and she tries to live one day at a time as fully as possible. She looks wonderful and we are happy for her.

I often see Rosemary Leone at our parish Sunday Mass. Her story is on page 105. Rosemary was one of our first clients when we established the House of Peace in 1981. She had been suffering from acute depression which she now realizes may have come about as a result of early menopause. Despite many problems over the past ten years Rosemary has managed to overcome all of them by maintaining a positive attitude.

Most recently Rosemary's husband, Bob, was diagnosed with Non Hodgkins large cell lymphoma. He first discovered it in his neck. During this time he received radiation and chemotherapy and also attended healing prayer services. When it was discovered in his liver, he continued medical treatment along with prayer. Rosemary and Bob are happy to announce that as of this writing the lymphoma is in complete remission. Raising a family of two children, along with a sudden change in Bob's job after 37 years could create depression in the staunchest of souls, but Rosemary believes that through her own experience of healing, she has learned to trust God with her life and her family on a deeper level.

Rosemary has gone on to attain her MA in Education. She told me that even though she lives a full and productive life, she has also learned self-caring in a healthy way. She asked me to pass on the message, "There is always help. Put your trust in Jesus." God is so Good!

Anthony Diffley, whose story is on page 175 of An Invitation to Healing, *was healed of a very large tumor in his nasal cavity. It had reached such an advanced stage that it was pressing into his spine and caused a loss of feeling in his face and eye. That was nine years ago and Anthony is still well. He has since married and he and his lovely wife, Toni, regularly attend the monthly Healing Masses at Blessed Sacrament Chapel, in Yonkers, NY. Since Anthony wrote his testimony for our first book, he discovered through the scans, that another healing had taken place. It seems the tumor had eaten some of the bone away in his cheek. The CAT scan showed that the bone had completely regenerated itself. Praise God! Anthony knows that by being vigilant over his mind and attitudes he will remain healthy; his faith in Jesus is very strong. A while back he decided to remove himself from a stressful job situation by starting a business of his own. During the writing of this book, in May 1991, the Diffleys completed their family with the birth of their first child, a son, Andrew Joseph. Anthony and Toni, we love you!*

Phyllis Ingrassia, on page 47, was healed of fibrocystic disease at a retreat we conducted in February 1985. She reported to us that she has had no further occurrence of the disease. She tells us that it has been seven years since her healing. In all that time she has never wavered from her faith in God's love for her and she maintains a strong belief in His healing power. Her heart is full of gratitude. Thank you, Jesus!

In the Gospel of John (6:68,69), Peter says to Jesus, "Lord, to whom shall we go? You alone have the words of eternal life. We have come to believe; we are convinced that you are God's Holy One." Those who have been touched by Jesus and his healing power can stand with Simon Peter and proclaim the same message. I have come to believe in a God of unconditional love who will deny His beloved children nothing. I believe in a God of Miracles. I want to proclaim from the housetops that God is only Good and much more than our finite minds can ever fathom.

Father Peter has written that all authentic healing is Spiritual Healing. It is the desire of my heart that you will come to understand the height, the breadth, the width, the awesomeness of the goodness of God as you read this book.

I love you,
Maryanne Lacy

Let us pray:

Oh, Lord, My God, it is with just the little bit of faith that we have that we place our trust and hope in your unconditional Love for us. We come to you this day with our hearts and our minds full of hope. Grant us the Courage that we need to risk and to make the decision to be healed. Grant us the grace to choose once again. If we have made wrong decisions about our health in the past, we ask that you help us correct our mistakes. Grant us the grace to persevere in prayer for you have told us in Holy Scripture to pray always. In the Name of Jesus, we ask to be freed from any false attitudes and beliefs that would block the flow of your healing Love flowing to us. We ask the Holy Spirit to be our helper and our guide in leading us to the healing and the forms of healing that would be just right for us. We pray for the medical professions and ask that the Enlightenment of the Holy Spirit may bring about a greater understanding of the need for the integration of Body, Mind and Spirit healing. We pray that we may know and understand Your True Nature so that we may come to know ours. All praise, honor and glory to the Father, Son and Holy Spirit now and forever. Amen.

The Miracle of Life

May 13, 1988
Father Peter and Maryanne,

Our daughter, Kathleen Elizabeth, was born on March 26, 1987. At birth, she was immediately transferred into the hospital's neonatal intensive care unit. Kathleen was known to have a potentially dangerous medical condition. Three weeks earlier, while in utero and during a routine sonagram, a large mass was detected in her abdomen. While doctors could only speculate as to the nature of this mass, they were certain that exploratory surgery would have to be performed soon after birth.

On March 31st, when Kathleen was five days old, surgeons removed a large tumor, about the size of a golf ball. They also removed her right adrenal gland, which was encased within the tumor. We were informed that this tumor was a neuroblastoma. (Neuroblastoma is known as the "silent tumor." It is a pediatric malignant disease that, once metastasized, takes the lives of most of its victims.) The doctors were confident, however, that they had removed all cancer cells. They chided us for worrying about our daughter and directed us to go home and enjoy our healthy child.

In July, three months later, we brought Kathleen back to the medical center for a follow-up sonogram. This sonogram revealed numerous neuroblastoma tumors throughout the baby's liver. We were directed to bring our child into the medical center to initiate chemotherapy the next day. We decided upon another alternative. Through our shock and grief, we made arrangements for Kathleen's medical care to be handled by a specialist at Memorial Sloan-Kettering. She was admitted the next day and remained there for two weeks. During that time Kathleen underwent intensive testing, which included liver and bone-marrow biopsies. These test results indicated that her cancer had metastasized throughout her liver and bone-marrow and was in the fourth (IV), or final stage. The prognosis was very poor.

While in the hospital, we decided that, upon Kathleen's discharge, we would take her to the House of Peace for healing prayer. We arrived at the healing service and walked to the altar when Fr. Peter McCall and Maryanne Lacy asked for the babies and children to come forward. In our anguish, we related Kathleen's history. We were anointed and the prayer team immediately began praying with us. Maryanne Lacy held Kathleen in her arms. She placed her hand over the baby's

liver and asked Jesus to heal her. Maryanne came to our home later in the week
for more healing prayer. We were showered with prayer, love and support. During the weeks to follow, Maryanne made
regular visits to our home and we continued to attend the Tuesday healing service.

In August, one month after being released from Sloan-Kettering, Kathleen had
another sonogram. The results indicated a
decrease in the tumor! Subsequent
sonograms showed an even greater decrease in the tumor. Finally, in December
1987, nine months after her birth, Kathleen was declared to be free of tumor. A
bone-marrow biopsy also confirmed this.
The specialists have no explanation for
this spontaneous remission.

We constantly thank God for this wonderful miracle! We praise Him for His ab-
solute love and goodness! Our Kathleen is
a beautiful, vivacious and loving child.

One year after her birth, Father Peter
McCall presided over the christening celebration of Kathleen. She had originally
been baptized immediately after birth in
the Intensive Care Unit. To date, we attend, whenever possible, Father Peter's
and Maryanne's healing service.

With love,
Rosemary and Tom Vassallo
Yonkers,NY

Chapter 2

RISE AND BE HEALED
OF BEING ABUSED

*"Though my father and
mother forsake me, yet will
the Lord receive me" (Psalm
27:10).*

As a healing prayer ministry, we are in constant
contact with hurting people. As we pray with these
people and listen to their stories, it has astonished
us how many speak about having been physically,
emotionally, or sexually abused as children. We are
seeing and hearing so much today about child
abuse. Public awareness of this issue has risen dramatically. In 1976, a Harris Poll showed ten percent
of the American population considered child abuse
a serious concern; the figure by 1983 had risen to
ninety percent. Here in New York City, the Lisa
Steinberg case was covered extensively by all the
newspapers and television news programs. More
and more people are willing to talk about their own
horror stories.

As someone who has been involved in a healing
prayer ministry for over ten years, I have been called

upon to try to heal many people who came from abusive homes and who today are suffering from the effects of such violence. It is important to address the issue of child abuse since it is more widespread than we might imagine.

The common denominator of all dysfunctional families is that they are shame-based. Family members are shamed by the irrational and compulsive behavior of a neurotic personality within the family. This is no more evident than in the case of physical, emotional, and sexual abuse. Whenever a child is slapped across the face, yelled at in a degrading way, or taken advantage of for sexual purposes, that child has been shamed. Anytime a child's boundaries have been violated by an intrusive adult who behaves as if the child were a piece of property, that child has been shamed.

To violate a child's boundaries means that the child's individuality and sanctity as a person has been compromised. Abuse occurs when an older and stronger person enters into a child's space unlovingly and uninvited. All abuse, whether it is done by commission or omission, (child abuse as opposed to child neglect) is a form of rape because a person takes advantage of a child's vulnerability, innocence, ignorance, and helplessness for his or her own purposes. To be abused means to be used in an unloving way with no respect for the personhood of the child.

Child abuse has been justified for cultural and religious reasons. Male children, for instance, have been castrated to retain their beautiful soprano voices for church service. We read about parents who believed that their child was "possessed" so they had to literally "beat the hell out" of the child.

It is important to point out here that certain forms of child abuse have been covertly approved and encouraged by our addicted society. When we hear people say that parents can do anything they want with their children and the court system backs them up, they are basically saying that children have no rights, which is an open invitation to abuse.

In the pamphlet, *The War on Children* (Hazelden, 1987), the author, Hal Ackerman, points out that people who abuse children come from every socio-economic, educational, and racial background. The abuse arises from a variety of reasons, but the primary one is the abuser's own childhood history. Child abuse, like alcoholism, can span many generations. Abusers learn to be abusive at home and teach it to their own children. He also points out, "Abusers often have little self-worth and low self-esteem. A large percentage of abusers are addicted to alcohol and other drugs. There is a tendency toward compulsive secrecy and internalized shame" (p. 6). This sounds like what we were saying in chapter one about shame being at the root of our destructive behavior.

If we saw an adult beating a child with a stick, we would probably intercede in some way. Physical abuse today is not as tolerated as it was in the past. We understand more these days that effective discipline does not require physical pain. But, if we observed an adult humiliating or calling a child derogatory names, we might feel distressed or disgusted, but we would probably not do anything about it. Both of these situations are forms of child abuse.

Emotional abuse affects the way we feel about ourselves, our self-image and our self-esteem. To be told by parents that they are no good, that they will never amount to anything, etc., makes them believe that what they are being told is true and they eventually act it out as adults.

However, the most shaming of all the abuses is sexual abuse. Here, the very ground of a child's being, the body, is attacked and taken advantage of. The obvious and overt form of sexual abuse is incest, where the helplessness and trust of the child is exploited by a family member for sexual satisfaction. The insidiousness of incest is that children are told not to trust strangers, but it is a trusted member of the family who takes advantage of them. There is more to sexual abuse than the exposure and fondling of genitals. All touch and looks which are sexually motivated are forms of sexual abuse. Anytime a child is "sexualized," made an object of sexual motivation, that child is sexually abused and, at some level, the child knows it. There is always trauma involved in sexual abuse which can have lifelong destructive effects.

There are subtle and covert forms of sexual abuse. The most widespread form is lack of information or misinformation about sex. In certain strict religious families, the rigid repression of sexual issues can lead to a shameful interpretation of sex with resultant unhealthy sexual inhibitions. We are sexually abused when we are not given healthy sex models to imitate, or when we are shamed because of gender jokes or teasing. We are sexually abused when there is no one to affirm and support us during the sexual changes of adolescence and puberty.

Sexual abuse does not take place between children themselves. When children show curiosity about their own bodies and the bodies of their peers, there is no abuse. Sexual abuse is always a violation of a person's rights and boundaries. Abuse takes place when people use their power and position over another to take advantage of him or her. There must be a victim and a victimizer in every form of abuse.

It is humiliating and shaming to realize that we have been victimized by abuse in our own home. It is so devastating because the children believe that they have done something wrong. They take the blame on themselves and think that if only they had acted differently the shameful behavior would not have happened. The first thing that abused children have to realize is that they did not do anything wrong. Also, they should not deny or minimize the behavior of the abuser. John Bradshaw says, "We will never be healed if we normalize the pathology within the family." We must "feel as bad as we really feel" so that we can eventually release it.

Forgiveness heals the effects of abuse as it heals everything. Forgiveness is not a cover-up for what really happened. The fact is that abuse in any form is not to be condoned or overlooked. One of the mistakes we can make in the healing process is to "forgive" too soon. This happens when we delude ourselves by saying that we forgive an abuser, when in fact there still remains pent up rage within us. We have to process our rage and anger because we have to realize that our boundaries have been violated. Anger, in this case, is healthy because it is telling us that we were actually violated.

No one is healed alone. Part of the wisdom and success of Alcoholics Anonymous is that it calls for each participant in the program to have a sponsor. The role of the sponsor is simply to be present for the participant in a loving and non-judgmental way. It is important that the sponsor be someone who "was there" himself or herself so that there is a joining of true empathy based on understanding. People who were abused as children need someone to listen to their story and allow them to ventilate their anger and shame in a healthy way. We do not have to be a therapist or social worker to help heal another person. Anyone with true compassion and understanding can be present with "unconditional positive regard," with no advice or suggestions, and simply give the other person permission to express how he/she feels without being shamed or judged. Abused children have been shamed enough by their family of origin. Now they need a "family of choice" where they can speak up for themselves without being put down again.

A friend of ours who is a psychotherapist attended one of our weekend retreats. At the end of the third day she said that more healing had taken place in that span of time than would have occurred in a year in a therapist's office. She observed that there was so much love and acceptance present in the group that it allowed people to work through issues in an accelerated manner. A climate of acceptance and affirmation which allows the hurts to surface so that they can be looked at and released heals abuse. As "healers" we are merely helpers who walk hand in hand with another person toward wholeness. In the process, we too are healed because a Higher Power (the Holy Spirit), who is present in each of us, is able to heal through us.

At some point in our adult life we must decide whether we want to hold onto the hurts of the past or let them go. Once we make up our minds to be healed, the Holy Spirit sends people into our lives to make up for what we missed as abused children.

ACOA has the expression, "It is never too late to have a happy childhood." One of the effects of being an abused child is that we lose trust in people. People we trusted in the past betrayed us; therefore, we find it difficult to trust again. But part of the healing process, under the direction of the Holy Spirit, is to draw people to us with whom we can once again trust and have fun. This new family may be a support group, a prayer group, or just new friends who call us beyond ourselves to new experiences. There is a risk in being healed and to risk new friendships is a leap of faith in the right direction. In many ways, "spirit is thicker than blood."

People who were abused by their blood relatives need to find their healing in new spiritual relationships. We said in Chapter One that all authentic healing is spiritual healing at the root. Adults who were abused as children need to form new spiritual relationships with people who will draw out of them the good that was always there but which never had the freedom to blossom.

I do not know how a person can maintain his or her healing without a spiritual life. There is a beautiful "child within" each one of us who was crushed by child abuse. That child is still there waiting to come out. All it needs is an atmosphere of acceptance and affirmation. The Holy Spirit sends us the right people with the right spirituality to heal us. He did it for me, and I know He will do it for you.

Father Peter McCall

Reflections and Sharing

RISE AND BE HEALED
OF BEING ABUSED

I know a woman who was repeatedly slapped on the face as a child. She had many emotional problems and in her twenties developed neuralgia on the left side of her face. When she came to us for prayer she would weep and her crying was that of a deeply wounded little girl. She told us that every time the laying-on-of-hands was applied to her face, she felt as though her soul was being healed also. John Bradshaw tells us that abuse soul-murders our children. The woman needed quite a number of treatments until finally the condition cleared up and her face was permanently healed. Praise God!

There have been many studies done on post-traumatic stress disorders concerning the Viet Nam veterans. Studies now show that people who have grown up in violent families display the same symptoms as those who had been in a combat zone. PTSD, otherwise known as Post Traumatic Stress Disorder, is the diagnostic term used for the symptoms experienced. The effect of this disorder is a delayed stress reaction. It is a form of survivor reaction to catastrophic stresses experienced in war. The characteristic symptoms, or emotional responses, correspond with the symptoms

37

resulting from violent family systems. Some of the common ones are: psychic numbing or emotional anesthesia, feelings of helplessness, dejection, withdrawal, anxiety and specific fears, hyper-alertness, exaggerated startled response, difficulty falling asleep, difficulty in concentrating, survivor guilt, suicidal feelings and thoughts. The list is endless. With the exception of survivor guilt, I have experienced every one of these emotional responses at one time or another. Thank God that through the past twenty years I have been healed of most symptoms through my involvement with healing prayer.

One of my favorite expressions is "Thank God for God". He sent to us a Savior, Jesus Christ. As Redeemer he has come to heal us and make up to us for the sins we commit against one another. It is my firm belief, because I have experienced it, that it is God's desire to make up to us through some form of tenderness for the violence that wounded us. We must open our hearts and believe in His love for us. For most people who have been severely abused as children the process of healing is usually lifelong. The kind of unconditional love that our Creator offers us through Jesus Christ and the Holy Spirit can only be received a little bit at a time. We humans are unfamiliar with divine compassion and love. We are familiar with punishment and condemnation. We have had people come to our healing services for healing prayer who are uncomfortable with being touched, and we honor that. We have had people pull away when we try to console them while they are weeping; they are just not used to being loved.

Father Peter has alluded to child abuse as being a boundary issue. He also referred to the perpetrator as being an intruder. In looking up the word "intrude" in the dictionary, I noticed that one of the definitions was: to act in improper disregard for the sacred or established nature. Our dysfunctional society and churches have handed down a sick set of rules to raise our children. How often I have heard religious people say, "Spare the rod, spoil the child." In the Hebrew Scriptures, there are two verses that religious people have used to condone beating a child: Proverbs 23:13,14 (NAB) reads, "Withhold not chastisement from a boy; if you beat him with the rod, he will not die. Beat him with the rod, and you will save him from the nether world." But we know from newspaper reports and television news that children die all the time from being beaten with instruments. However, in the New Testament, Jesus goes beyond that view. Matthew refers to Jesus according to the prophecy of Isaiah, "The bruised reed he will not crush; the smoldering wick he will not quench" (42:3). The tenderness of Jesus for children is evident in the Gospel of Luke, "They even brought babies to be touched by him. When the disciples saw this, they scolded them roundly; but Jesus called for the children, 'Let the little children come to me. Do not shut them off. The reign of God belongs to such as these'" (18:15-17).

Many people don't even realize that they were victims of abuse. I recently became aware of this when I had a conversation with two elderly women. The first one told me that her father used to chase her with a stick when she was "bad." "But it was probably because I deserved it," she said. The second woman said that she would often get slapped in the face for "mouthing off." She too felt she probably deserved it.

Our dysfunctional society has even used Mother Goose nursery rhymes to advocate child abuse. In my ignorance I never gave it a thought when I recited these rhymes to my own children — "There was an old lady who lived in a shoe, she had so many children, she didn't know what to do. She gave them some broth without any bread, and she whipped them all soundly and sent them to bed." Recently a woman, Kittie Malloy, gave me a book called **Father Gander** *(Advocacy Press, 1985.) its messages redeem many of the old ones found in Mother Goose. His version of this nursery rhyme is: "There was an old couple who lived in a shoe, they had so many children they didn't know what to do. So they gave them some broth and some good whole wheat bread and kissed them all sweetly and sent them to bed. There's only one issue I don't understand, if they didn't want so many children why didn't they plan?".*

Dr. Doug Larch, who wrote **Father Gander,** *thinks we have a responsibility to see to it that our children grow up unbiased toward another's age, color, sex and religious preferences. He believes that the singsong qualities and resulting enchantment of many of the old nursery rhymes lulled people into ignoring the occasional messages of violence, sexism and discrimination. I think this is a multi-generational problem. Much work is needed to undo the ways in which we feel, think and act toward children. Dr. Doug Larch is one* *example of the many people who are trying to make a difference. I read recently that Beverly Sills, the renowned soprano, is working toward educating people on the need to respect one another and pass that respect on to our children. She writes, "Everything this great country is, and hopes to be, is inextricably intertwined with the future of its children. We must love all children, not just our own"* (McCall's Magazine, *May 1991*).

I had a great deal of difficulty preparing this particular commentary because of the subject. I had been through so much personal healing in this area that I didn't really want to go back over it again. For most of my life before the healing process I could not deal with the subject of child abuse. I could not read about it or watch anything concerning it on television. One evening many years ago, I was watching a television movie. Suddenly, without any warning there was a severe act of violence against a woman on the screen. I ran from the room in fright and sobbed uncontrollably. I surprised myself, to say the least, but I knew then that I had to address the issues of child abuse in my own life. I did not want to believe it happened to me. I was trying to live a perfect life. I didn't want anyone to know I was less than perfect lest I be shamed again. I know now that this is all part of the behavior that comes from abuse. We try to cover up our shame by creating an image that makes us acceptable. My experience was enlightening because it made me aware that I needed help. The help came in the form that God knew was best for me. I found a spiritual family through various prayer groups. The twelve step programs had not yet mushroomed as they have now, but through these prayer groups, I was led to warm and safe people where I felt loved.

Father Peter writes that we are sexually abused when there is no one to affirm and support us during the sexual changes of adolescence and puberty, but even worse is when parents knowingly choose not to protect a child from sexual molestation. I know countless women who have shared such experiences with Father Peter and me. They have recounted how they had been sexually abused by a relative, a pastor or a friend of the family, and when they told their mother they discovered her to be totally unsupportive. In fact, many have told us that their mother would usually ask them to keep it a secret from their father for fear that he would do something to harm the perpetrator. It is beyond my comprehension that a mother would protect the abuser rather than her own child. The most primitive instinct in animals is to risk their own lives to protect their young.

Twelve step programs have been instrumental in breaking the secrecy barrier associated with sexual abuse. I know a brave young woman from a distant state who went public with her story of incest. The particular area where she lived has Incest Survivors Awareness Week. She assisted many women and men to realize the scope of the problem and helped them recognize that they are not crazy nor are they alone. Most recently, in the June 10, 1991 issue of **People Magazine,** *Marilyn Van Der Bur, Miss America of*

1958, revealed to the world her pain in dealing with incest. It was shocking. Her millionaire father had molested Marilyn and her sister for thirteen years. Her life had become a devastation, but through professional help she was able to get her life together again. As a result of her recovery she has started the Adult Incest Survivors Program at the Kempe Center in Colorado. Marilyn's goal is to make the word incest speakable and to take away the stigma we attach to it.

According to the fact sheet on the after-effects checklist for survivors of sexual abuse, most victims suffer from gynecological problems, gastro-intestinal disorders, headaches, joint aches, arthritis, eating disorders, alcoholism and drug abuse. Many of the women who have come to us for prayer for the healing of cancer in the area of gynecology have been sexually molested. We usually suggest that along with healing prayer, they also seek some form of psychotherapy. These are only some of the physical symptoms. There are other manifestations as well such as: skin carving, self-destructiveness, suicidal thoughts, paralyzing depression, as well as sleep disorders. Childhood amnesia is very common in childhood sexual abuse.

With God all things are possible. With Jesus Christ as our Redeemer and Healer even something as vile and vicious as incest and sexual abuse can be healed. With the grace of God we have ways to help each other. We are living in a wonderful age of healing. I see around me countless forms of healing modalities that are available to anyone who needs them. I also thank God and

Our Loving Savior, Jesus, because as Redeemer he can and does make up to us for the loss of love in our lives.

Each person is born as a sacred being, created in the image and likeness of God. It is the mission of the healing ministry to reveal their sacredness to God's children. In our retreat work we attempt to do this in various ways.

On the retreats, the teachings are geared to undo the beliefs and images of God that are destructive, as well as to re-train the retreatants to feel better about themselves. Most people who attend healing retreats have little or no self-esteem, although they don't realize this. It is most evident when we try to encourage people to make positive statements about themselves, for example, "I am lovable," or "I am kind." For the most part, people are quite uncomfortable with this exercise. Many healings have occurred when our retreatants were able to look at their innate goodness. Many break down and weep for the first time in years. Often we use various methods to reveal the reverence we feel for people. We have ceremonies where we bow to one another in the oriental fashion. We acknowledge our reverence for one another. We also use incense as a sacramental. We incense our retreatants to remind them of their holiness. This is a very humbling experience for many because they are not used to being treated with such high regard.

In our book, An Invitation to Healing, *we write about the healing that came from our spiritual family. It has been our experience in the healing process that a spiritual family will be sent to help heal us. In Matthew 12:48 and Mark 3:33, Jesus addresses the crowds say-*

ing, "Who is my mother, who are my brothers?" Then extending his hand toward his disciples, he says, "There are my mother and my brothers. Whoever does the will of my heavenly Father is brother and sister and mother to me." In Luke he answers the question by saying, "My Mother and my brothers are those who hear the word of God and act upon it" (8:21). In healing, we need to listen to the voice of the Holy Spirit to lead us to a source of healing that will be suitable for us. The spiritual family we are led to will depend on the needs of our particular journey. It may be a prayer group, a support group or a twelve step program. We need to grieve and forgive our past in a safe place. We need to give permission to one another to share our pain and allow the little child within to experience unconditional love and freedom from danger.

At our seminars many people have expressed regret when they realized that the family traditions that they were brought up with were sometimes unhealthy. The retreatants ask us how they can undo the harm that has arisen as a result of being misguided. Father Peter and I tell them that the best thing they can do for their children and families is to seek recovery for themselves. Step number eight of the Twelve Step Program refers to making amends to people we may have harmed. We need to be willing to take responsibility for the wrongs committed against others. In step nine we are told to make direct amends to such people wherever possible except when to do so would injure them or others. I believe that the power of the Holy Spirit will reveal to us who, when, and how we are to do this. For instance, a young woman came to us in great anguish. She had an abortion years ago and it still gave her emotional pain even though she had confessed it. She had gone through psychological therapy and thought she had forgiven herself, but still she suffered from self-recrimination. As I prayed for her, I thought the dimension that was lacking in her recovery was reparation.It should not be in the form of more self-punishment but in restitution - making up to a child in some way the loss of a parent. I asked her to go into prayer and ask the Holy Spirit to guide her in this. Perhaps she was being called to become a big sister to an inner-city child or to help minister to abandoned babies. For the first time in a long time she felt at peace about this and went about seeking the guidance of the Holy Spirit.

Father Peter and I feel a responsibility, as members of the healing ministry, to do our part in working toward ending child abuse and abuses of all kinds. This work is my way of making amends for the damage I have done in the past even though I was ignorant of it at the time. I have chosen, with the help of God, to intercede, to fast, and to pray for the healing of others. I know that maintaining my healing depends on reaching out to others. It is only by the grace of God that I have found health in body, mind and spirit. With Father Peter, I join in encouraging you to trust in God and in yourself.

I love you,
Maryanne Lacy

Let us pray:

Heavenly Father, The Scriptures tell us that it is not your will that any of your little ones come to any grief. For many of us this is quite a revelation. Grant us the grace to believe in You as You really are. Truly You are a God of Love. It must be Your will that all children be treated with fairness, justice and respect. We ask that the minds of all humankind waken to the fact that all life is sacred. Jesus taught us to pray when he told us that "whenever two on earth agree on anything in my name it will be granted."

So we join together now with the children of the world and ask in the name of Jesus that there be an end to child abuse. We pray for the protection of children everywhere. Oh, Lord Jesus, we ask that you assign angels to watch over and protect our children. We also include all unborn children in the womb in this prayer. We truly thank you for the gift of life. Help us and grant us the grace to forgive ourselves for any part we played in not respecting life.

We present all child abusers to you, Oh God. We ask in the Name of Jesus that they will have an awakening and seek the help and healing they so sorely need. We thank you for the greater understanding in segments of our culture where there is the awareness of the rights of human individuals. We ask for healing of the little child within each one of us.

Make up to us through the love that pours out from the Heart of Jesus and His Most Blessed Mother so that we may receive the nurturing that we feel we need. We affirm that we are precious children of the Most High God and nothing can harm us. We are protected and we are safe in the loving arms of the Angels and Saints. We praise You and thank You, for we know you have heard our prayer. All Glory and Honor to the Father, Son and Holy Spirit. Amen.

A Psalm of Healing for Adult Survivors of Childhood Sexual Abuse

Lord, God, I come before you in great torment. I am sorely in need of your help. I long to be close to you but in my confusion I don't even know where to turn. I can't seem to find my way. I need you to take me by the hand and guide me. There are times when I can't even feel. At times I don't even know who I am and even worse, Oh God, sometimes I feel as if I am crazy. I need someone to tell me that I'm not crazy. I need someone to let me know I am okay. God, do you really know my innermost thoughts? The Bible says you do. Then you must know how deeply troubled I am in heart and mind and spirit. Lord, I must confess that I felt I was all alone. That no one could possibly understand what I am going through. My heart is full of sadness and grief. I long for the innocence that was once mine but was taken from me. Fear and trembling overcome me. Unknown horrors overwhelm me. I yearn; yes, how I yearn with all my heart to find shelter from the anguish that pursues me. I yearn to flee from the violence and the raging storm that engulfs me. Will I ever find the peace and tranquility that my soul seeks. Sometimes, in the recesses of my mind secrets arise, dark secrets, and once again I am anxious and afraid. There are times when I think death would be a comfort and I am tempted to do away with myself. Oh, Lord, whom can I trust? Can I place my trust in you? But, Lord, it was someone I trusted who defiled me. I cannot forgive. I am at a loss for I do not know how to forgive. Yet, Jesus tells us that we must forgive. Show me how. Show me how to trust again. Show me how to choose once again to trust you.

I feel so empty inside. There are many times when that emptiness is too great a burden to bear. I try to fill in the emptiness in destructive ways and the emptiness always returns. I remember reading that Jesus spoke to the woman at the well. He told her that whoever drinks from the water that He gave would never be thirsty again. I, too, desire to drink from this water that Jesus offers so that I, too, may never feel empty again. Fill me, oh, God with this Living Water that I may have the gift of new life.

At night I lay upon my bed and sleep eludes me. I am haunted by shadows and unknown terrors. I long for the respite of a peaceful sleep but it escapes me and I long for the light of a new dawn. Lord, save my soul and my mind from its ceaseless wandering. Let my heart rest in you. I long to be unfettered from the chains of fear that keep me in bondage. Only your love can liberate me. In the shelter of your kindness I take refuge. I choose to believe that your love is greater than my pain. I call upon your faithfulness to grant me greater faith and trust in you. I call upon your compassion to comfort me. Awaken my body and my soul to your saving grace.

Lord, what am I to do with the shame? I feel so guilty. Do I need to forgive myself? What do I do with my anger? I am so angry. How do I deal with all these emotions without destroying myself? Do you have the answers? Can you show me the way? I need to make right choices for myself but I also need guidance. I have made so many mistakes and I am tired.

Lord, Jesus, you were put to shame. You harmed no one and yet your were stripped naked for all the world to see and hung on a cross. I know you understand for you were exposed and yet you never condemned your perpetrators. Grant me this same excellence of grace so that I, too, may be free from animosity. By your Divine influence and example I, too, may be reprieved from the desecration I feel in my life. Though I feel oppressed from all sides, I have decided I would rather be happy and so I choose to place my trust in you. Lord, God, I long to be near you and never be separated from you. You are so magnificent and glorious. I will choose to Praise you all the days of my life. I resolve to believe that I am a Precious Child of God, heir to the throne of Heaven. I prefer to commit myself to be healed and I am determined to see it through with your help and the help of the Holy Spirit. With Jesus and the Holy Spirit, I will be guided and directed towards my goal of health in body, mind and spirit. I thank you, Dear God, for having heard my prayer. Amen

Chapter Three

RISE AND BE HEALED
OF GUILT AND SHAME

> *"There is no condemnation now for those who are in Christ Jesus" (Romans 8:1).*

We made the bold statement in chapter one that the shame we learn in our dysfunctional family is the "tap root" of all our problems and diseases. In this chapter we want to examine shame in more detail and see how insidious it can be. There is a debate among ACOA counselors as to whether there is such a thing as "good shame." John Bradshaw maintains that we need a "little shame" to keep us humble and to keep us from believing we are God. He says that we need enough shame to keep us from running naked through the supermarket. Others maintain that shame, in any degree, is destructive and has no redeeming value. Shame, as we will talk about it here, is always unhealthy. The "good shame" that some people talk about is really wisdom or common sense.

We define shame as an all-pervasive feeling and belief in our own inadequacy, inferiority, helplessness, unworthiness, condemnation, and incompetence all rolled into one. This is the shame that eats away at us and will eventually kill us if it is not healed.

Shame Is a Multi-Generational Problem

It is important to understand shame as a multi-generational problem because we tend to blame our immediate family, school, and church as responsible for the bad feelings we have about ourselves. Shame has been around a long time. It is interesting to note that "original sin", as taught by the Catholic Church, is an "inherited sin," that is, it is not a sin that we committed, but one that was done to us by our ancestry. When did all of this begin? I believe that it all began with our first parents. When we read Chapter Three of the Book of Genesis, we see how Adam and Eve "hid" from God because they were afraid. Why were they afraid? Because they were naked and ashamed. Shame goes all the way back to our first parents and has been propagated through the generations ever since.

Shame is the one feeling we share with every member of the human family. We can say that the entire human family is dysfunctional because it has propagated shame to all of its members. Cultures and religions have used shame throughout the ages to control and manipulate.

What Is It About Shame That Is So Destructive?

To say that shame is at the root of sickness and disease is to say that what we believe can hurt us. Shame is a belief. Jesus said many times, "Your faith has made you whole" (Mt 9:2). It is just as true to say that our faith can make us sick. Faith is always powerful and it can heal or hurt us. Fear is an act of faith. It is a belief that something evil or bad will come upon us. It is negative faith. We see it expressed in the Book of Job, when Job says, "Whatever I fear comes true, whatever I dread befalls me" (3:25). Fear, because it is an act of faith, can bring about the very thing it fears.

Shame is a belief that was taught to us by our addicted society and the dysfunctional family. The difference between guilt and shame is that guilt makes us feel bad about something we did, while shame makes us feel bad about who we are. Shame is a belief that we are somehow defective, that there is something radically wrong with our being. Is it any wonder that shame can set us up for all sorts of negativity in our lives?

It must be mentioned here that our shame is like an iceberg — very little of it appears above the surface. Most of our shame is suppressed and lies beneath the level of our consciousness. We can easily deny our shame and pretend that we really feel good about ourselves. However, there will be times when our defenses fall apart and we come face-to-face with it. The belief that we are no good brings with it various corollaries which have many negative effects on our health and well being. Let us examine some of these effects.

What Shame Can Do To Us

Shame is a belief that we are not worthy of good, so we are not surprised when misfortune comes our way. Being of Irish decent, I am aware of the Irish belief that when things are going well, it is the time to worry. An example of this Irish belief was expressed by Senator Patrick Moynihan when President John F. Kennedy was assassinated. He said, "What did you expect? Everything was going so well. .. There is no sense in being Irish if you don't believe that the world can break your heart." Shame teaches us that God will eventually "get us" and give us what we really deserve — punishment for our sins. My own father had a stroke a few years before he died. He rationalized it by saying that he had many good and happy years and that it was only right that he suffer a little before he died so he could go right to Heaven. Shame can set us up for sickness by seeing it as something we deserve and expect.

Our shame doesn't allow us to think too highly of ourselves. Our addicted society teaches us that pride is the root of all evil. The worst sin we can commit is pride. Our experience in the healing prayer ministry has taught us just the opposite. It is not pride that is the root of all evil, but a devastating self-hatred. The only reason that we would choose what is evil or harmful to ourselves is because of our own feelings of self- condemnation and lack of self-worth. Our behavior at times may appear as pride in the sense that we might try to dominate others. But, we would never have a need to prove ourselves better than someone else unless we really didn't believe it ourselves. We hide our true feelings of inferiority behind the mask of superiority. What appears as pride is really lack of self-esteem.

The evil that we do to ourselves and others is a result of our shame. We would never attack ourselves or others unless we felt bad about ourselves. The purpose of addictions is to numb the pain we feel about ourselves. Addictions are smoke screens behind which we try to cover up our true feelings. So much sickness and disease are simply manifestations of a death wish — a form of self-punishment. The death wish may not be conscious because so much of our shame is unconscious.

We were once asked to pray with a psychiatrist who had developed cancer. As was our custom, we asked him if anything significant happened around the time the cancer was detected. His answer was "no." We prayed with him a number of times, but his condition only worsened. Then, almost by accident, his wife told us that just before the cancer was detected he was sued. It seems that he was treating a patient who was suicidal and the patient committed suicide. The parents of the patient sued him. It was shortly after this that he developed cancer. Yet, he insisted that nothing significant had happened just before he developed cancer. It was obvious that he was in complete denial and that, at some level, he was committing suicide himself. It showed me that even a psychiatrist did not know what our shame can do to us.

Since shame teaches that we have no intrinsic value, we search for it outside ourselves. Love and acceptance are seen as conditional and must be earned by our perfect behavior. Perfectionism is taught in the dysfunctional family. Shame also teaches us that we can find our value only by helping others, even to the point of assuming responsibility for their happiness and becoming their savior. This co-dependent behavior sets us up for stress and conflict which eventually runs down our immune system. We set the stage for psychosomatic and physical sicknesses. Research into dysfunctional families reveals that often it is the co-dependent spouse that becomes physically debilitated or dies even before the chemically-dependent spouse. The constant strain of always trying to please or rescue others becomes too much for the body to take.

Another form that shame-based co-dependency can take is a belief in martyrdom and victimhood. So much sickness and disease can be traced to a belief that we must sacrifice our lives for others. When individuals have so little self-esteem themselves, they look to other people and causes to give all their energy and attention. Sometimes these people are praised as saints when all the time it's their own shame that compels them to think more about others than themselves.

At our healing services, we often see people who are obviously racked with pain from arthritis. When we ask them what they want us to pray for, they insist that they do not want prayer for themselves, but for their children who are not going to church. They think it selfish to pray for themselves. They accept their sufferings as "carrying their crosses" so that others might benefit from it. Such an attitude appears noble, but it has more to do with shame than with altruistic motivations. Jesus told us to love others "as" we love ourselves; not more than we love ourselves.

Shame can set us up for sickness and disease to be used as a way to get even with others. This represents passive-aggressive behavior. Shame-based people often have difficulty in expressing anger or disappointment. They believe that if they express their anger openly, they will lose the love and respect of others. So, rather than openly and honestly expressing their anger, they "swallow" it and take it into their bodies. The suppressed anger is expressed as sickness. The sickness becomes a covert statement, "Look what you have done to me." Our experience has taught us that often sickness and disease are nothing more than suppressed rage.

Some of us are not ready to accept shame as our major problem because we have developed clever defenses against it. We mentioned that shame is like an iceberg and that the greater part of it lies beneath the surface of our consciousness. Our shame is so dreadful and hideous that we believe that if we ever exposed it or looked at it, we would be annihilated. This is why so many people think that if other people really knew them inside-out, they would be rejected. It is because of shame that we will go to such extremes to look good and make a good impression. At the core of our being we don't believe in our goodness so we present a "social-self" to the world.

The first defense we all use against our shame is denial. We have discovered that denial is the biggest obstacle to healing. Anyone who has had any experience with Alcoholics Anonymous knows that the greatest deception that an alcoholic uses to maintain his drinking is denial. There is an expression in AA, "Take the cotton out of your ears and put it in your mouth." We are not ready to be healed unless we overcome denial.

Since we began our healing ministry we have always taught that pain and suffering are not God's will. We do not believe that God sends us pain or suffering to punish us, purify us, or test us. God is only good, and only good can come from God. However, pain and suffering are human inventions which we need to tell us something needs to be fixed. Pain and suffering are the body's way of saying that something is wrong and that change is necessary. They are calls for love.

The only way that we can ever overcome our denial is if the pain gets so great that we eventually cry out for help. The only way our defense of denial will be overcome is if we experience a nervous breakdown, a serious accident, or a mid-life crisis. God does not send these. They are the natural consequences of our beliefs, attitudes, and behaviors which we have never challenged and which we presumed were true. A mid-life crisis is a spiritual experience of disillusionment. The belief system that we had accepted for so long begins to fall apart and our shame, which the system was created to hide, begins to get exposed.

Our defense of denial will eventually fall apart because the pain gets so intense. Some of us have different thresholds for pain which accounts for the fact that some of us do not have to hit bottom before we "come to our senses" (Lk 15:17). However, we are not quite ready to be healed. In our arsenal of defenses against the truth, we have yet another major weapon. When our denial falls apart, we rely on projection to save us from looking at our shame. Projection is a defense that does not directly deny the pain or suffering, but rather makes someone else responsible for it. Projection saves us from looking within by assuming that the cause of our misery is outside our own mind.

Projection defends shame by finding scapegoats to blame for it. It says that the reason we feel bad about ourselves is because of our dysfunctional family, our religion, our school, our environment, our genes, or anything outside ourselves. At this point we have not found that sense of powerlessness which represents our willingness to take the first step of a twelve step program. We still believe that blaming others for our problems gives us power over them. We can absolve ourselves from any guilt and shame because we found another to blame. We believe that finding someone else on whom to place the responsibility for our guilt frees us from it. We feel a temporary release from our shame by pronouncing someone else guilty.

Like the defense of denial, projection also begins to fall apart. We thought that we had solved our problems by blaming others for them, but it did not work. We still feel as bad as we did before. Projecting our guilt onto someone else simply backfired. There is a good psychological reason why this happens. We eventually realize that when we project condemnation onto others, it returns to us. This is what Jesus so clearly taught when he said: "Stop judging and you will not be judged. Stop condemning and you will not be condemned. Forgive and you will be forgiven. Give and gifts will be given to you. . . For the measure with which you measure will in return be measured out to you" (Lk 6:37,38). We soon learn that what we project has a boomerang effect and returns to us in a similar form. We thought we freed ourselves from shame by hurling it at another, but all that it did was return to us. Projection solved nothing. We still feel as troubled as we did before.

The only way to heal shame is through forgiveness, but forgiveness is not a cover-up for what really happened to us in our dysfunctional family. Authentic forgiveness does not include either denial or projection. "Healing begins where blame leaves off."

In our first book, *An Invitation to Healing,* we described the forgiveness process in a chapter called "Healing Our Relationships." This particular chapter has received the greatest reviews. Today, we still consider our message of "radical forgiveness" to be the heart of our healing ministry. Since it is so important, it is necessary to repeat some of the themes of that message especially as it applies to the healing of shame.

The first step in the radical forgiveness process is to overcome denial and projection. We bring the problems into ourselves where we can do something about it. We will never be healed as long as we pretend the problem does not exist or that it will go away if someone else changes. To place our healing onto what someone else does or does not do is to give our power away. To make our healing dependent on what another does is another form of co-dependence. Seeing anyone else outside ourselves as a savior or scapegoat sets us up for failure. Healing is never based on what another person does. We tried that and it didn't work. We must bring the problem to the solution which is always within our own mind.

Certainly an addicted or abusive parent contributed to our shame, but if we wait for that parent to change before we begin the healing process, nothing will ever happen.

The second step involves the realization that we can choose to accept healing or not. We do not have the power to heal ourselves, but we can decide whether we want to maintain the beliefs, attitudes, and behaviors that are contributing to our misery. Some people insist on holding onto beliefs in victimhood, martyrdom, and holding other people responsible for their misery when all these beliefs do is recycle the anger and shame and keep them in the same rut they were in before.

We are not denying what other people did to us, but we are affirming that we have the right to choose an interpretation of the past that will free us from its effects. We don't have to keep rerunning the old tapes in our mind. We have the option of seeing the past differently in a way that does not propagate anger or shame. This is the heart of the second step. All we need do is be willing to let go of any grievances we hold against others and be open to another way of looking at the past.

The only reality that the past has is in our mind. The past dwells in our mind, not as a fact, but as an interpretation. Only the present moment is real. The past is gone and the future has no existence. How we see the past and the future is our own choice. We must assume responsibility as to how we interpret the future. The second step in the forgiveness process is simply taking responsibility for our basic human freedom. We choose our attitude toward life at any given moment.

The third step reveals the difference between a psychological approach to healing and the approach we take in spiritual healing. The third step is not ours to do. We need Someone to heal us Who is in a better position than we are to see our problem differently and Who can empower us to change our minds. We call this Someone the Holy Spirit. We believe that He is our Inner Guide Who will show us how to re-interpret our problem from a different point of view so that we can choose "a better way" to go through life.

Once we have expressed our willingness to see our shame differently, we invite the Holy Spirit to show us options that we would never have thought of on our own. How He will do this is not our concern. Our concern is to let go of control over the healing process and withdraw any investment we have in any particular conclusion.

We have said often in our healing ministry that it is not so much what we do that heals us as much as it is what we undo. In the healing of shame, it is not so important that we do anything, but it is important that we be willing to let go of our own preconceived ideas and let ourselves be healed by a Power that is not our own. This Power is within us.

Not everyone sees the world the same way. So, too, not everyone is healed in the same way. The way shame is healed depends on how we interpret ourselves in relationship to others and to God. It was in relationships that we learned shame, and it will be through relationships that we will be healed. The addicted family system taught us shame. No individual is to blame for this, because we all bought into the same system. To be healed from shame, we have to go outside the system that taught it and adopt a new one. We learned shame, so we can unlearn it. Shame was not given to us by God. It was handed down to us by generations who bought into an addicted society. With the help of the Holy Spirit, we can withdraw from that thought system and accept another one which brings peace and joy.

Once we decide to give our shame over to the Holy Spirit, He will guide us to interpret ourselves, others, and God differently. He will do this in very imaginative ways. Usually, He does it by sending people into our lives who send us messages different from the ones we heard as a child. He provides a "new family" in which we are free to be ourselves without censorship or condemnation. However, we must be open and willing to accept these new messages. This is the risk of healing we spoke about in the last chapter.

We will unlearn shame as the Holy Spirit leads us more deeply into meditation and contemplation. We will get in touch with a "Self" that we never knew existed. Prayer will become a quiet time rather than a time of anxious petition and painful contrition. We will now hear the truth about ourselves and this truth will set us free (Jn 8:32).

Shame is basically a spiritual problem because it has so much to do with how we see ourselves in relationship to God. Once we realize that what we believe about ourselves is not what God knows about us, we gradually let go of self-condemnation and shame. As we begin to grow spiritually, our sense of shame begins to decrease. We begin to see ourselves as we truly are, sons and daughters of an unconditionally loving God Who would never shame us. In this realization is the healing of shame.

Father Peter McCall

Reflections and Sharing

RISE AND BE HEALED
OF GUILT AND SHAME

Ugly shoes will always be reminiscent of the feelings of shame for me. I had long skinny feet, I was told. Hard to fit, I was told. The only pair of shoes in all of New York that could help these feet were the ugliest that could be found. My classmates in school would say, "How come you have to wear those shoes?" To top it off, I was also embarrassed and self-conscious because the clothes I was made to wear weren't much better. I tried to hold my head up high but my inferiority complex was winning out. I resented deeply that I was forced to look different. I thought brown lace-up oxfords should be banned. Of course, I was told there were children in the world who didn't have any shoes to wear so I should be grateful. I remember one Easter, when I was about fourteen years old, I managed to convince my stepmother to buy me a pair of low, high-heeled, navy blue pumps. My father took one look at them and demanded that they be brought back. I was so disappointed and the flat-heeled black shoes I ended up with made me feel even more ashamed. My feet looked like boats in them. The public high school where I was sent was one of New York City's largest. My shame and inferiority only worsened as I was made to wear the brown oxfords to high school. I was so embarrassed by my shoes and clothing that I tried to make myself invisible in school.

When one is shamed, it is extremely painful at any age; but, when one is a child it feels like helplessness. I can remember despair settling into me at about that time. There just doesn't seem to be anything a child can do about the situation when severely dysfunctional adults are in charge. These feelings get buried like a sleeping dragon only to surface at some future time. I didn't begin to realize how deeply ingrained in me this problem was until a few years ago. I never seemed to be able to buy shoes that fit me properly most of my adult life. I bought shoes that hurt my feet and I usually developed blisters and corns. They were usually plain shoes except for special occasions.

When I was giving a retreat once, a retreatant, who happens to be a gifted lady, felt she was meant to pray for me. I felt comfortable with her and so we joined in prayer. She had an insight that I should take better care of my feet and indulge myself by purchasing better shoes. She had an image of many different styles and colors of shoes in my life. You can imagine my astonishment. The Bible tells us that God cares about the hairs on our head, but it doesn't mention feet. Although, when I think about it, they did a lot of foot washing back then. I truly thank this dear woman for listening to the Holy Spirit and sharing her insights with me. Isn't it marvelous that we have such a personal caring God? Who but the Holy Spirit would have known? Only a personal Savior would have come up with an idea that would have healed me of these memories of shame. Of course, being an obedient child of The Most High God, I became quite free about choosing shoes from then on. I was a wee bit uncomfortable in the beginning when I would enter a better shoe store and try on shoes of a higher quality or of greater value than I was used to. But now I am totally at ease and free of guilt when I shop for shoes. I don't suffer from sore feet anymore either.

About a year ago, I was taken by surprise when a woman came to us for prayer who was suffering from the same complaint. She shared with us how her mother squelched her attractiveness and made her wear plain clothes and brown oxford shoes as a child. And I thought I was the only one! We have prayed with this woman for release from feelings of shame and, of course, it eventually comes back to the basic lesson of forgiveness. In the end, it is the act of forgiveness that becomes the most important choice we must make if we truly want to be well.

Shame affects our sexuality. All of us, depending on our personalities, have different ways of dealing with shame about sex. I got the definite impression from my family that being attractive was a threat. I also received messages from my father that being attractive meant I was possibly in danger from the opposite sex. I learned very early never to look seductive in public and I have carried that over to this day lest I be labeled shameful and bring disgrace upon myself. The healing work I am doing now guarantees that I will never allow myself to dress alluringly for fear that I open myself to defamatory gossip and so feel shamed. At any rate, I feel safe in this role and it is all right at this stage of my life.

"Shame, shame! Everybody knows your name!" This is a familiar phrase to almost everyone. The crossed fingers pointing accusingly towards you with a "tsk, tsk, tsk", and a "shame on you" is also familiar. It seems as though it has permeated every area of our lives. "You should be ashamed of yourself" is something I have heard all too often. This childhood abuse and the resulting shame extends from family life right on into the classroom. A lovely young woman came to us for prayer with intense feelings of low self-esteem. During prayer she had a flashback to when she was in kindergarten. She had to go to the bathroom very badly but the teacher ignored her raised hand until she finally wet herself. The teacher reprimanded her publicly and shamed her in front of the entire class. Thanks be to God and this woman's desire to get well. Through healing prayer and forgiveness she is now learning that she is a precious child of God.

Many of us have suffered physical and emotional abuse in the classroom. One very angry lady told us that when she was "bad" in class the teacher would lock her inside the clothes closet. She had come from a severely alcoholic home as well so we had to pray with her for a long time before she was able to work through her rage and finally come to a point where she was willing to forgive. This particular woman has amazed Father Peter and me by the remarkable transformation in her appearance.

I have an unpleasant memory of being brought into the principal's office for talking in the classroom. While she was scolding me, she kept shaking her fountain pen at me and the ink was splattering all over my face. I felt so small and helpless. I have gone through so many processes of forgiveness in my life that I understand now why Jesus tells us we must forgive seventy times seven. Life is a lesson in forgiveness and it "ain't easy."

I heard John Bradshaw say that our body is the ground of our being. A friend shared with me that when she thinks of shame, she associates it with her body. Normal curiosity about her body as a child was met with secrecy or a strong suggestion that it was wrong. She eventually got the idea that her body and her sexuality were dirty. I think most of us can identify with that.

We have been called as healers to be the means where God's broken people can approach Jesus in faith and experience God's Unconditional Love. Our role in this work requires a great deal of compassion. We have committed our life to bringing peace, solace and comfort where there had been shame, guilt and abuse.

I know that something wonderful is going on in the world today. Regardless of the negative media reports, there is much goodness going on as well. I believe we are in an age of healing. Today, more than ever, people are willing to speak out against injustice. There is a massive mushrooming of twelve step programs. Through these programs people are finding the courage to uncover the crazy family systems that constitute society. Most of us thought we were alone because there was so much secrecy associated with dysfunctional and alcoholic families. Now we know we are not in isolation and there are many people who care about our well being. We have more options today; more choices. Thank God.

The grace of disenchantment hit me like a bomb when I was in my early thirties. My pain was very great and I wasn't even surviving. I felt I was smothering and in danger of perishing. In fact, I was dying but to a completely false and illusionary existence. If I had any sense of self or identity it was indeed a stranger to me. I was the people-pleaser par excellence. Co-dependence wasn't even a word back then. When my pain became too much to bear and I finally cried out to God in despair, the Lord of Love was able to filter His healing through the gradual opening of my defenses. In time, when I was ready, Jesus Christ, Son of the Living God, espoused me to him with the Fire of His Divine Love. I was filled with a love that can never be described in earthly terms. I have not been the same since. Nor do I want to be. I was transformed with a peace from Heaven for the first time in my life.

As time passed I began to experience a new awareness about myself. I had known for quite a while that all was not right in my marriage. I didn't know myself well enough to understand what to do about it. I sought some professional advice, but no one seemed to know quite what to do. Father Peter points out that besides the defense mechanism of denial there are two other biggies - projection and scapegoating. I can assure you from experience, all three major defenses are rampant in dysfunctional families.

Father Peter is right when he writes that healing begins where blaming leaves off. Thank God, I had entered into a spiritual journey and was able to gradually make my way through the maze of confusion. I was led by the Holy Spirit to an excellent therapist who was also a spiritual man. I can only say that when I chose not to play the game of projection and scapegoating any longer, my marriage fell apart.

There are strong feelings of guilt and shame when a Catholic marriage falls apart. It was particularly hard for me because I had been trying to live up to the image of a perfect Catholic family. I can recall a time when I was self-righteous. I told my friend and neighbor that I felt sure the reason marriages don't last is because people don't have enough faith. I added that I felt they also didn't work hard enough or commit themselves to making the marriage work. There is a saying, and I keep it in my office at home as a reminder, "Make sure your words are sweet and tender for tomorrow you may have to eat them."

No one in the church community seemed to know how to deal with my failing marriage. Guilt and shame were a constant merry-go-round. Blaming was the name of the game. During the time I was in therapy, I came to understand that no one person is to blame for the end of a relationship. If there is any fault it has to rest on the dysfunctional society in which we live. I don't know how anyone can rise from the shame of a broken marriage without the help of a Higher Power.

Through prayer and meditation and with the prayer support of my friends, I was able to go through what could have been a stormy and traumatic period of my life with the least amount of anxiety, guilt or shame. A divorce is like a death and actually is the death of a family. There is always a great deal of grief and anger to work through. I have five children and I know they went through a great deal of pain and confusion during those years. I believe they have come to peace with it in their own way. I give them a lot of credit because at this time they are all doing well.

The healing came for me through my willingness to choose to forgive. I had to turn my emotions over to the Holy Spirit and constantly let go. In Luke's gospel Jesus speaks from the cross, "Father, forgive them; for they do not know what they are doing" (23:34). In hindsight, I saw that my ex-husband and I had not fully realized what we were doing to each other. As I reflect, it is a wonder to me that we stayed together as long as we did.

Forgiveness is not a one time decision. We may have to forgive again and again. Sometimes forgiveness is like water dripping on a rock; we may not see the results right away but one day the realization comes that the hurt no longer has power. It probably was hardest to forgive myself since I have always been toughest on myself. Jesus has been healing me of this issue for a number of years. I recall sometime ago, when I was in the midst of reproaching myself, an inner voice interrupted and said, "Maryanne, you see yourself through the eyes of admonishment but I see only that you need love". I knew this was Jesus — "A bruised reed He shall not crush" (Mt 12:20). There are times in social situations when the topic of divorce arises and I am tempted to feel ashamed but I know the signs now and I see it as just that, a temptation. I usually turn it over to the Holy Spirit and let go. As the saying goes, Let Go and Let God. It seems to me that life has become a constant letting go. I find my life works better when I do. What I have discovered is that there is no shame in being human and making a mistake. The error is to think that oneself is a mistake or a disgrace.

I love you,
Maryanne Lacy

Let Us Pray:

Blessed Be The Lord in whom I place my trust. Oh, Lord, God teach me to do Your will. May your Holy Spirit guide me in the ways of Truth. Lord, I have been put to shame and I have come to you with my pain. Only you, Oh God, are kind and just. Only you can bless my life with the comfort I need. Help me this day to see myself as you see me. Help me to believe in myself and in your love for me. Show me how to love myself and others as you love. Show me how to forgive. Show me how to forgive myself and how to forgive the people in my life who have hurt and shamed me the most. Lord, I need to let go of the burden of guilt I carry in my heart. I long to be free. You are my hope. In your great kindness rescue me and never let me be put to shame again. I pray to you, my God that you will protect me all the days of my life.

My heart has been broken many times and sometimes I feel as though no one could ever love me. I humbly place myself before you knowing full well I need your Love. I need your healing power to bring me peace. Jesus tells us in the Bible "Come to me, all you who are weary and find life burdensome, and I will refresh you. Take my yoke upon your shoulders and learn from me, for I am gentle and humble of heart. Your souls will find rest, for my yoke is easy and my burden light." With this wonderful message in mind I ask Jesus, so gentle and kind, to lift the burden of guilt and shame from my heart, so that I, too, may find rest. I acknowledge that the Lord withholds no good thing from me. I believe I shall be completely restored with the grace of God the Father, Jesus Christ and the Holy Spirit. May the Glory of the Lord endure forever. Amen.

Chapter 4

RISE AND BE HEALED
OF ANGER

> *"Keep in mind dear people:
> let everyone be quick to hear,
> slow to speak, slow to anger,
> for a person's anger does
> not fulfill God's justice"*
> *(James 1:19 & 20).*

As we talk about being healed from the effects of living in a dysfunctional society, we must deal with the issue of anger. If we came from a family that was abusive or addictive in any way, we should not be surprised that we are angry. We probably would not have survived in such a family if it were not for our anger. Anger was our defense and protection at a time when we had few options to fall back on. Anger was the only way we knew how to express the fact that our needs were not being met and that our rights as an individual were not being respected.

There is an anger that does not need to be healed. For the sake of clarity, we will distinguish between anger as an emotion and anger as a decision to attack another. As an emotion or feeling, anger can be helpful because it is a signal that something is wrong and calling out for attention. We get angry for a reason and we should listen to the message that our feeling of anger is offering to us. It is the emotion of anger that Saint Paul is talking about when he says, "Be angry, but do not sin; do not let the sun go down on your anger" (Eph 4:26). Saint Paul is saying, look at your anger. Do not deny it. Like pain, anger could be telling you that you have been hurt and should do something about it.

In a dysfunctional family, our anger was probably telling us that our boundaries had been violated. Anger is a response to abuse of any kind. When someone takes advantage of our vulnerability and uses us in an unloving way, anger can tell us that our personal inner space has been violated and that we have been treated in a disrespectful, degrading way. Without our anger we would have no boundaries, no sense of "self" as an individualized person with a right to be respected. Without our anger we would become "door mats" and allow other people to victimize and take advantage of us. Our anger tells us that an injustice has been done and that correction is in order. Abuse of any kind is an invasion of privacy and our anger can become a protection against further abuse and humiliation.

Anger as an emotion is a necessary part of our survival repertoire. One of the ways that our dysfunctional family controlled us was to tell us that anger was a sin and that no good Christian (or whatever) child should ever get angry. We were told the words of Jesus, "Whoever is angry with his brother is liable to judgment. . ." (Mt 5:22). What was so frustrating about this experience is that they told us these words in anger. One of the rules of a dysfunctional family is that the parents can get angry, but the children must not. This is one example of the double-messages being sent out in an addicted family.

Anger as an emotion does not need to be healed unless it begins to control us. As long as we take responsibility for our anger, that is, "own our anger," and use it as an informational service from our psyche, we do not have to fear it. It is only when we use our anger as a justification to attack another and project onto someone else the cause of all our problems, anger becomes our master rather than our servant.

Anger can be very tricky. We can learn very early in our lives that anger, especially in the form of a temper tantrum, can get us what we think we want. We can use anger to manipulate and control others. In fact, some people have been so successful at using anger to get what they want that they become addicted to it. These people become rage-aholics. They learn to use their anger not only to control people, but to protect themselves from intimacy. Just as alcoholics use alcohol to numb their pain and as a defense against looking within for solutions to their problems, so rage-aholics use anger as a way of keeping their problems outside themselves and thus guarantee that no solution will be found.

As long as anger is working for us, we will never question or challenge our investment in it. It is only when it begins to backfire and bring more pain than release that we will seek help. At some point we begin to realize that just venting our anger does not solve problems. We may feel better when we release anger at another, but it's only temporary. We might begin to suspect that maybe our anger is having side-effects in our body. We might begin to see a possible relationship between the temper tantrum we threw the night before and the migraine head-ache we have the next morning. Just as we can have a "hangover" from too much alcohol, we can also have one from too much anger.

Part of our dealing with anger has to do with learning how to manage it in such a way that we can be assertive enough to express our feelings without making an aggressive attack. We must learn to let others know exactly how we feel without demanding that they change to please us. This involves accepting responsibility for our anger and being able to express it without attack or retaliation. This is the "nuts and bolts" of working through anger.

Fighting, criticizing and blaming others only assures that a problem will never be solved and that change will never take place. Simply repeating old patterns of behavior that have never really worked before only protects the status quo and acts as a smoke screen to conceal the real issues behind our anger. We will never find the reasons why we get angry as long as we hold others responsible for it. As long as we continue to play the game of who is right and who is wrong, we get caught up in a vicious cycle of defense and attack which never gets resolved.

The resolution of anger only comes when we accept our feelings as our own and are willing to look within to clarify issues that our anger has aroused. In order to do this without guilt, we need a safe place where we can express our anger to someone who will not condemn us. "We have to feel what we need to heal." Sharing our anger with someone else who will not attack us or tell us what to do about it is the best way to let our anger come to the surface so that we can look at it and eventually let it go. We need space where we can "step back" and observe our anger without condemnation so that we may search for the interpretation within ourselves which gives rise to such angry feelings. We don't see facts in the world; we see interpretations. We need to quiet ourselves to such an extent that we can discover the root interpretation that has such anger attached to it. When we reach this stage of processing our anger, we are now faced with a choice as to what we want to do with the interpretation. Anger is not the problem. Anger is the effect. We no longer have to work with anger, but with the thoughts and beliefs on which the anger is based. We can now ask ourselves, "Do we want to be right or happy?"

The problem with anger is that we can so easily justify it. In a recent incident in the Crown Heights section of Brooklyn, NY, a Hasidic Jew accidentally ran over a nine-year-old black child. This touched off such anger in the Black community that a gang of Black youths attacked an Hasidic student and knifed him to death. For the next two nights there was violence in the streets with many police officers being injured trying to restore peace. These Hasidic Jews and blacks had lived next to each other for over sixty years. Although there had been minor incidents throughout the years, there had been nothing compared to the violence which erupted over this incident. Both sides felt they were justified in their anger.

The blacks demanded that the driver of the van which struck the child be arrested and prosecuted, but no charges were filed against him. One black teenager was arrested for the death of the Hasidic student although a whole crowd had attacked him. Both the Jews and the blacks insisted they were right and that violence was justified.

The bottom line of all this violence and rioting is the belief that anger is a natural emotion and that acting out anger gets us what we want. It is also based on the belief that retaliation is always justified and that satisfaction can be achieved by inflicting suffering or punishment on another. As the newspapers and television played up this incident in Crown Heights, it soon became apparent how insane everybody was acting and that the whole situation was destined to happen. This brings up a point which I believe is at the heart of acted-out anger and violence: We are already angry before any incident happens that apparently makes us angry. Nothing that happens to us makes us angry. We are already angry and we find an excuse to vent it. This point can be verified by an incident that happened in Brooklyn.

New York's Mayor Dinkins, himself black, was on the scene with leaders of the Jewish community who did not approve of the violence and who were pleading for peace. This means that not everyone in either the black or Jewish community agreed with the anger or violence. This tells me that some people were already angry and waiting for a situation to happen so as to justify it, and that other people were not already angry so they saw the violence as useless and non-productive. Whether one chose violence or peace is predetermined by the state of mind of the individual.

All of this has important ramifications in regard to the healing of anger. I believe that anger is a subjective judgment and is determined not by an external event but by the interpretation of that event in the predisposed mind of an individual. Anger then is a decision we have already made before anything happened to us. When something happens that can justify this anger, we explode and blame our anger on the event that happened. Actually, the event was neutral and could have been interpreted in any way we chose. The fact that we chose anger simply manifests the anger that was already within us. Our behavior reveals our interior disposition at the time the event happens.

If we are already angry before anything happens to us, where does this anger come from? There is a part of us that sees ourselves unfairly treated by the world, our families, and more deeply, by God. This gives rise to a radical anger which we carry with us and try to deny or hide. It can surface at any given moment, however, because it is subtle and slippery. In my experience of praying with people for healing, I have become aware of just how much anger there is in people toward God They would firmly deny such anger at God because of fear of retaliation from God or because they would not want others to think they were mad at God. Many people have images and expectations about God that are simply not true, but they believe they are true. Then when God does not live up to their expectations, anger is the result. Those people who claim to be militant atheists are really people who have an image of God that has not worked so they deny His existence.

We should not be surprised that so many people are angry at God and blame God for their troubles. We live in a society that refers to nature's violence, such as lightning, floods, earthquakes, etc. as "acts of God." It is presumed in our addicted society that if things go wrong that cannot be explained, it must be God who is doing it. God always gets blamed for the unexplainable. The irony about this is that in our day we can now explain many things which were blamed on God in the past. What we once interpreted as "Divine wrath" (thunder and lightning) is now easily explained in grade school science books. However, because of our guilt and shame, we tend to interpret tragic events as a punishment from God.

Seeing God as wrathful and as the cause of our misfortunes is common in many religions. Just a few years ago, when pilgrims were going to Mecca for a feast and the weather was extremely hot, an air conditioning unit in a large tunnel broke down with thousands of people in it. The people in the tunnel began to panic and stampeded over one another to get out. The result was that thousands died. Religious leaders explained the event as "God's will." The problem with this is that God is used to explain acts of violence. Once more, we receive a double message. We are told to be compassionate and forgiving, yet God can be angry and violent. People end up thinking that if God can be angry so can they. Anger is justified in the name of God.

Once we have an angry and violent God, we will have an angry and violent society. Anyone can claim that their acts of violence are inspired by God. We know of many child abuse instances where the child was almost beaten to death to drive the "devil" out of the child. If we hope to heal anger and violence in our families and community we have to re-examine our whole concept of God. This is why I believe that all healing is ultimately spiritual healing because it always boils down to our interpretation of God and His role in the healing process.

I would like to propose that anger, as a decision to attack another, is insanity. If I am correct, anger would be impossible in God because then God would be insane. The reason I say that anger to attack is insane is because it is based on the misperception that we can attack another without attacking ourselves. Just as it is insane to believe that the suffering of another person can alleviate our pain, it is just as insane to believe that we can attack another with no ill effects upon ourselves. Jesus gave a great psychological teaching when he revealed that giving and receiving are the same (Lk 6:37-38). He taught that what we do to other people, we do to ourselves. If we attack others, we attack ourselves. If we forgive others, we forgive ourselves. In other words, whatever we send out to others returns to us in the same or similar form. This was also taught by Jesus in the Garden when Peter wanted to defend his Master with violence. Jesus told him, "Put your sword back in its sheath, for those who live by the sword will perish by the sword" (Mt 26:52).

The insanity of our addicted society is revealed in the belief that retaliation brings justice. It is important to note that one of the Laws of Moses, which

Jesus changed, is the Law of Retaliation (Lex Talionis) "An eye for an eye and a tooth for a tooth" (Mt 5:38-39). Jesus says, "Offer no resistance to evil." To an addicted and dysfunctional society non-resistance to evil is total nonsense. Even the Christian churches have paid little attention to this teaching. We have always been able to find justification for our counterattacks upon others. But Jesus knew exactly what he was saying and he intended his followers to take him literally on this issue. Jesus knew that violence breeds violence and that the only sane way to stop it is to stop being part of it.

Jesus's teaching on non-resistance does not mean that we do nothing about the violence in our midst. It means instead that we do not fight anger with anger and propagate the defense/attack syndrome. We can learn a lot about how to handle anger and violence from the movement known as Tough Love (For information write: Tough Love, P. O. Box 70, Sellersville, PA 18960). This is a support group for parents of incorrigible family members. The basic premise of Tough Love is that you can do anything necessary to control an undisciplined family member as long as the motivation is love. The steps needed to correct a situation may vary, but the motivation should not arise from the need to retaliate. Someone once said, "If you are not part of the solution, you are part of the problem." This is true in regard to anger. If we respond to anger with anger, we are part of the problem. If we can "step back," and check our motivations, we will be in a better position to be helpful.

Saint Augustine once said, "Love, and do what you will." This phrase could be interpreted to mean that we can do what we want to do, but before we act there must be love in our hearts. That love will inspire us to do what is most helpful and beneficial in any specific situation. Jesus was right when he said, "Do not resist evil." He meant that we should not become part of the evil. We shouldn't get sucked into violence because someone else is violent. Anger which attacks is never justified because it perpetuates the very thing we are angry about. That's why I say it's insane.

The entire issue of anger can be complex and difficult. The emotion of anger can be very productive when it is used as a call for change and growth. Ultimately, the healing of anger is the same as the healing of any problem - forgiveness. Forgiveness is not the condoning of wrong-doing, but the relinquishment of the belief that attacking another will solve the problem. Forgiveness is not something we actively do, it is rather something we undo. We undo, or let go of the belief that attack gets us what we want and that we will not be happy until someone else suffers. This is the insanity of anger. To be healed, we must question our previous ways of solving problems and look for a better alternative than attacking to express anger.

I do not believe that anger is natural to us. I say this because we were created in the image and likeness of God and anger and retaliation are not attributes of God. "God is love" (1 Jn 4:16), and love has nothing to do with anger and attack. Anger is not our root problem. Anger is a defense which we use to stop us from looking at our real problem which is fear. We fear rejection, abandonment, and loneliness. These are our real problems which we will discuss in the next chapter.

Father Peter McCall

Reflections and Sharing

RISE AND BE HEALED
OF ANGER

Anger is an ugly emotion that ranges from mild irritability to fury, which is rage so great it resembles insanity. When this country was engaged in the Persian Gulf War, the issues of rage, fury and insanity seemed to be rampant in the world. It was as if the principal of retaliation that Father Peter has just addressed was being shown to us as a visual aid on the screen of life in an dramatic way. On television we saw the scenario of defense, attack, good guys, bad guys, kill or be killed. The world had gone insane with hatred. It didn't take me long to realize that what was being projected from the Middle East happens every day on a smaller scale in the scheme of life. We have neighbors right in our own neighborhood who are attacking other neighbors.

There was a time in my life when I played the game of attack and defense with expertise. I thank God for helping me to understand my anger. Through the years of healing prayer and therapy, I have learned to deal with anger and become more free. In my upbringing, anger was probably the only dominant emotion experienced. I think it was a way of controlling the family. I grew up with a fear of angry people, and yet I seemed to set myself up in relationships with very angry people. I was later to discover levels of rage that were lying deep within me just waiting to explode, and I was afraid of that explosion. Using anger as a problem-solving technique was passed down from generation to generation in my family. All the men in my family are angry people. For many years I was afraid of men. It took years of inner healing work and therapy to help me uncover my fear and especially the fear of my animus (the male side of my psyche/personality). I had projected this fear of the masculine onto the image of God as Father. I was afraid of God. I believed He was capable of punishing me and, in due time, I had to admit that I was enraged at God. The breakthrough occurred at my Baptism of the Holy Spirit, in 1973; this set the stage for a miraculous healing in my life.

Through this experience, I discovered a personal relationship with Our Lord and Savior, Jesus Christ. Through his consistent love and the guidance of the Holy Spirit, I have know that God is Love and that God exists only to love. Through spiritual insight, I became aware that I had been angry at God for doing things He hadn't done; I only perceived He had. My anger at God has been abated and I can't begin to tell you what a relief it is. I felt as though I had been in prison and had finally been released. I have come to the awareness that whenever my anger arises, I must deal with it immediately and nip it in the bud, otherwise I suffer unhappy consequences. However, the healing of anger is an ongoing process.

My bouts of anger have diminished greatly over the past few years and I thought I had been doing well for a while. One day, not too long ago, it reared it's ugly head to let me know I had more healing work to do. The lesson came in the form of a maintenance man when my heating system needed repairs. I had always done business with this particular company and was pleased with their work. The day I called, a different man came and I thought he was newly hired. He seemed quite pushy, very talkative and downright rude. But I excused his behavior. He fixed my upstairs heating system and presented a very high bill, which I paid, attributing it to the higher cost of living. The next day my downstairs heat was not working and, again, he presented me with a large bill. This time, since I did not have the money, I asked him if he could wait a while for payment. The next day, the heating system was still not working and I called again. After repeated efforts to fix the heater plus another bill, I decided to make an inquiry. I was told this man was the new owner of the company. On his last visit, he informed me more work had to be done and the cost he quoted was outlandish. I finally spoke up. When I became assertive and complained, he became defensive and began raising his voice in anger right in my home. I told him, in no uncertain terms, that he was completely out of line and had no right to speak to me in such a manner. I said his business practices were questionable and I was going to report him to the Better Business Bureau. Needless to say, I was furious. I wanted to give this fellow one good charismatic kick. When he left I was steaming mad, but I tried to be reasonable and Christian about it. It wasn't working though, so I did what I usually do and vented my anger to someone who cared. Meanwhile, I developed a headache and stomachache. I asked some friends to pray for me and lay hands on me for healing.

I started this chapter by stating that I feel anger is an ugly emotion. I will go even further and say that I don't even think it is a natural emotion. The only natural emotions are those associated with the realm of the Holy Spirit. Yes, while we are in this world we will experience anger but we can, through prayer, rise above it and through the help of the Holy Spirit defuse it so that it will no longer have power over us. While we are on this spiritual journey we are called to a higher level of thinking, but we should never deny our human emotions. Through meditation, contemplation and centering prayer, we can reach a level of awareness that helps us to see others differently. Anger can have a wretched effect on us and can cause many physical ailments.

As I sorted through my feelings, I felt justified. My anger was telling me that my boundaries were being violated. I realized that I still needed healing in regard to aggressive men. I was pleased, however, to have had the opportunity to stand up for myself. I was never good at that. Usually I felt intimidated and would elect to back off. Through prayer and in peace I came to the decision that I had to make a formal complaint to the Better Business Bureau. I carefully thought through my motivations for doing this. I had to be absolutely sure I was not doing it out of a desire to retaliate. I knew, in all fairness and justice, that this man had to awaken to the consequences of his actions. As a consumer, I thought it only right that the public be made aware of unfair business practices. I made the complaint in peace.

One of the best things I have ever done for myself was to attend an assertiveness training program. I think our dysfunctional society has placed a burden on women. We are not supposed to get angry, especially "nice" Christian women. Women are supposed to be nurturers, caretakers and peacemakers. Unresolved rage, over a long period of time, can create serious physical illnesses, even cancer. I highly recommend assertiveness training courses for all women and men. It is a powerful tool in helping deal with the issues of anger and boundary violations. The program teaches that we all have basic human rights.

A priest I know was surrounded by a group of people at a meeting. They were engaged in conversation. A woman came up to him and in order to get his attention pulled at his shirt and then on his arm. Much to my surprise, he turned to her and said, "I did not give you permission to do that." He then turned back to the group and continued the conversation. I was amazed that this man was able to assert his rights and not care what anyone else might think. Assertiveness training teaches that we have the right to say no. This is very hard to put into practice especially for those in the ministry of healing. A woman once put me through a great deal of mental anguish because she felt I did not spend enough time praying with her and she wasn't getting well fast enough because of me. She tried to make me feel guilty and, of course, I became angry. She was violating my boundaries.

I shared my story of a bout with breast cancer in An Invitation To Healing. *I likened unresolved anger to an ice ball that was in the form of a tumor in my breast. My anger had been disguised under the face of innocence, but in reality, I wanted to get even with a lot of people for letting me down. This all happened in the years following the breakup of my marriage. This is why I believe it is so important to see a therapist, counselor or psychiatrist while trying to be healed of a life-threatening illness. There are many layers of unresolved issues lying underneath the surface. The sooner we face our anger, deal with it, and get on with the healing, the better. I can't say enough about the value of healing through the laying-on-of-hands. I must emphasize, though, that just as we should be particular in our choice of doctors, so must we be with someone who claims to have the gift of healing through the laying-on-of-hands. Through this gift, God's love and energy can permeate layers of unresolved hurt in a short period of time.*

The subject of how to deal with one's anger comes up most often at our retreats and workshops. A great deal of time is spent on how to work through anger. The great majority do want to be healed and get on with their lives in peace. It is important to note that we must work through the issue of anger before we can forgive. Forgiveness is a process that brings us peace. Many

*people do not realize that they need to respect the fact
that it takes time to heal anger and to move on.*

*Recently I went to Florida with two of my daugh-
ters, Mary and Kathy, and my granddaughter, Jessica.
We were on the beach all morning and at noon went
back to our room for lunch. We left all our belongings
on the beach. When we returned some children were
playing with Jessica's pail and silver shovel. We paid
no attention until they started to walk off with them. I
asked them to bring them back, but the little girls insisted they belonged to them. But the youngest with
them, a little boy, said, "Oh, no, you found them, they
were right there on the sand," pointing to where we had
left them. The girls resisted and swore that the pail and
shovel were theirs. They were so convincing that even I
almost believed them, but Kathy and Jessica knew better.
The parents of the children were nearby, and when
Kathy approached them, they began to argue about it.
Kathy didn't want an argument, so we explained to
Jessica we would get her another pail and shovel. Father
Peter's words came to me, "Would you rather be right
or happy?" Mary, Kathy and I considered the matter
and felt we had to make an adjustment in our attitude
for the sake of peace, even though we knew the truth.
We did buy Jessica a new pail and shovel, even better
than the one she had. All of us felt we had done the
right thing.*

*Father Peter says he also had to make an adjust-
ment in his attitude in order to gain peace of mind.
One of his pet peeves is when he is sitting in his car,
waiting for the light to change and a driver behind him*

beeps the horn. This used to cause him to lose his peace of mind and he would get angry. Once, when this happened, he said the thought came to him, "People do what people do. There are people who honk their horns in this world and that is their problem." Now when a horn-honker is in back of him he says, "People do what people do," and lets it go.

Another subject that always seems to arise on our retreats is the dry drunk syndrome. It is amazing how many families have lived with this for years and did not know it had a name. I refer you to two pamphlets put out by Hazelden Educational Materials (Box 176, Pleasant Valley Road, Center City, MN 55012-0176), entitled The Dry Drunk Syndrome *and* The Dry Drunk Revisited, *by R. J. Solberg. I first heard the term thirteen years ago when I attended a talk by a counselor who was active in AA. I was struck deeply because I saw a pattern in my family members and friends that explained a lot to me. Dry drunks are people who may not be drinking, but have not yet dealt with their alcoholic personality problems. The people I knew who fit into this category were not out-and-out alcoholics but would binge on raging. Father Peter alluded to the rage-aholic as someone who is addicted to rage. I have been a witness to this and it is not a pretty sight. The rage-aholic can be quite frightening. They lose all control and become temporarily insane. I don't have to tell you of the destruction and havoc it causes, especially to children. They can develop the same symptoms as those children who live in a war zone. Addiction to rage is a difficult problem for families. Usually they will need*

*outside help such as counseling or twelve step programs
to see their way through it. Many treatment centers have
developed programs designed to deal with the complica-
tions of the dry drunk for the family as well as the
alcoholic.*

*We must never underestimate the power of Grace
to transform lives. I remember once when I was going
through a great deal of anguish in a relationship. I was
very angry with the other person, yet I felt so unhappy
and uncomfortable with my anger. I went to God in
prayer and asked Him to please take the anger I was
feeling in my heart. Much to my delight I found it
vanished instantly. My peace of mind was restored and
I marveled over it. I praised God for such a miracle. I
couldn't even remember what I had been angry about.
I have tried this method since and it hasn't worked. I
usually have to work through the anger, deal with it,
forgive it, and then let it go. I know that only with the
grace of the Holy Spirit will I be restored to the Peace
that passes all understanding. So can you.*

I love you,
Maryanne Lacy

Let Us Pray:

Father in Heaven, I am far from peace. My heart is in great turmoil. I am so upset. I need to let go of my anger, yet I am not able to do so. There are so many confused thoughts twisting and turning inside of me. Lord, I was betrayed. I am enraged. I want to hurt back but I know that this is not the answer. I need to find my way again. Help me, Oh, God to be free. Lord, what is it in me that seeks vengeance? My hurt is very deep. Only your love can relieve me. I am in great anguish and my heart cries out to you for help. I need to understand why I am so angry. I bring to you in love my little child within who is still reacting. I ask you to comfort this frightened child who felt so powerless. This child was terrified of the anger of others and lived in fear of unpredictable rages. Lord, God, I need to know how to deal with my anger appropriately. With the Holy Spirit as my guide, I will not be afraid to look within.

Help me to be responsible for my actions and see that my anger is a call for change. Teach me to express my emotions in a healthy way. I cannot allow my anger to control me anymore. It is too destructive. I need your help to see differently. Grant to me the grace to make an adjustment in my perception. I long for tranquility and respite from the rage that engulfs me. Dear Jesus, I ask you to see to it that justice is brought about in this situation (here, mention the situation. . .). I choose to surrender all that I am feeling to you now. I humbly ask that you remove from my heart and mind all desire to get even. Help me to forgive. Set me free from the darkness of depression. With your healing light bring peace and joy back into my life. I love you and praise you now and forever. Amen

Chapter 5

RISE AND BE HEALED
OF FEAR

> *"...for God has said, 'I will never desert you nor will I forsake you.' Thus we may say with confidence: 'The Lord is my helper, I will not be afraid. What can anyone do to me?'" (Hebrews 13:5b & 6).*

In praying with people for healing, we have discovered that the greatest obstacle to healing is fear. Fear immobilizes us to such an extent that we become unwilling to move forward, to think new ideas, to seek new experiences. Fear can have such a hold on us that we fail to see new opportunities for physical, emotional, and spiritual growth. There is no healing without change, but fear paralyzes us and prevents us from accepting change into our lives. We can become addicted to our fears. There are people who are "worry-holics." They need something to worry about in order to feel alive. The invitation to healing is perceived as a threat. In discussing the healing of fear, we must first clarify exactly what needs to be healed. There is a type of fear that helps us to be on guard for situations that can potentially harm us. This awareness of possible dangers is part of wisdom and prudence and does not need healing. There is also the "fear of God" which The Scriptures speak about. This Biblical fear is really awe or reverence before the majesty of God as Creator. It is not servile fear, but rather the wonderment and amazement appropriate in relationship to the Divinity. This type of fear does not need to be healed.

The fear that needs to be healed is that painful feeling or uneasiness of mind that comes from anticipating evil or that chronic anxiety that always expects the worst to happen. It is expressed so well in the familiar song, "Old Man River," which says, "I'm tired o' livin' and scar'd o' dyin'." Fear can actually become a state of mind which controls all of our decisions. What can make matters worse is that fear becomes a self-fulfilling prophecy and can actually bring about the very thing it is obsessed with. Fear of rejection by others, for instance, can actually set us up to be rejected. We teach others how to treat us, and our fears can send out messages that others pick up and act upon accordingly. With Job, we say, "What I feared has come upon me; what I dreaded has happened to me" (Job 3:25).

Where does fear come from? We were not created by God with fear. Fear is not a natural emotion. Fear is something we learned from our dysfunctional society. When we were taught, either explicitly or implicitly, that we were really no good and that we had to earn or merit our goodness through the approval of others, fear took root in our being. Once we were shamed, fear of being exposed was born in us. And once we accepted ourselves as flawed and defective, fear of punishment became inevitable. What compounds the fear is that we were taught that even God is displeased with us. We had to earn God's approval too or else condemnation awaited us. A God of vengeance is an essential part of a dysfunctional society which needs to keep its members guilty in order to control them. Our expectation and anticipation of punishment is what fear is all about.

Karl Menninger once said, "Fears are educated into us, and can, if we wish, be educated out of us." If we want to be healed of fear, we have to understand the nature of fear. Fear is essentially an act of faith. It is a decision we make as to how we will interpret what we see. Often, when Jesus healed, he said to the person, "Your faith has made you whole" (Lk 8:48).Faith is always powerful. Faith can heal us, but it can also hurt us. The object of our faith makes the difference between whether it is helpful or harmful. For example, if we have faith in the goodness of God and our own inherent goodness, good things will come about. If we have faith, however, in an avenging God and in our own "radical wrongness," it might bring about the anticipated punishment which is the natural conclusion of such belief. Fear is faith, but faith turned against ourselves.

Fear comes in many forms, but the underlying content is always the same. The essence of every form of fear is shame expressing itself as self- condemnation. We all try to deny this shame by covering it with defenses and projections. Addictions are smoke screens and distractions behind which we hide our shame. All the violence in the world is nothing more than attempts to project blame onto others for the feelings of self-hatred we hold about ourselves. Eventually all defenses break down. They do not last forever, and that is what we fear the most. We fear the "day of judgment" when we will be exposed before all the world and our "sinfulness" will be revealed for all to see.

What maintains our fear is the belief that there is no alternative to it. We believe that eventually we will get caught and there is nothing we can do about it. Fortunately, there is a way out. There is an alternative to fear. This alternative suggests that what we have believed about ourselves is simply not true. We were told a lie, and we went along with it. No one person or group of people were responsible for telling us this lie. It has been passed down from generation to generation. The problem was that nobody questioned it. The lie was taken for granted and incorporated into our societies, cultures, religions, and family systems.

The lie that we were all told was that we are no good in and of ourselves and that we had to earn or merit our goodness through the approval of others, including God. We have all tried to do this, but it hasn't worked. We never quite made it. We could never do enough to please those who would confer goodness on us. We were in a "no-win" situation in which we were "damned if we did, and damned if we didn't." We were doomed to be damned. There was no way to escape the punishment we deserved.

Into this hopeless situation comes the alternative. There is a different version of the story we were told and it has a completely different conclusion. The version suggests that we are radically good, and that the mistakes we have made have already been corrected. We do not have to earn or merit our goodness because we received that at our creation. Any mistake we made is not greater than God's love and God's answer to our mistake is not punishment, but healing. Healing is correction without punishment. Fear is groundless because God is Love and Love does not attack or hurt. This different version of the story reflects the words of Saint John the Evangelist, "There is no fear in love, but perfect love drives out all fear because fear has to do with punishment and so the one who fears is not yet perfected in love" (1 Jn 4:18). Love and fear are mutually exclusive because they are based on two mutually exclusive premises. Love is based on the premise that "God is love" (1 Jn 4:16) and that love does not condemn (Rom 8:33). Fear is based on the premise that God is an avenger and that someday we will receive the punishment that our radical wrongness deserves.

I realize that the alternative version of our story has not always been taught by our churches. In fact, one of the reasons why our churches have added to the dysfunction of our society is that they have supported and encouraged the same technique and methods used by the dysfunctional family to maintain and propagate shame and fear. The churches, in many instances, were part of the problem and not the solution. This is clearly seen in the historical approach taken by the churches to alcoholism. The alcoholic was called a "sinner," a "moral deviate".

The alcoholic was told he was guilty and guilt meant punishment. The thought of punishment leads to fear. Fear needs defenses and a good defense is to deny the problem by getting drunk. The solution offered by the churches maintained the vicious cycle or attack/defense and kept the problem alive.

Fortunately, in 1935, an alternative was offered. This alternative viewed alcoholism as a disease to be healed, not as a sin to be punished. It told the alcoholic that he/she made a mistake which could be corrected by the Twelve Step Program. No longer was the situation hopeless. The alcoholic was not doomed to be damned. Fear was driven out by the love of the members who reached out to one another in a non-judgmental way. A disease is a call for help, not condemnation. Once condemnation was taken away, fear disappeared.

There is great resistance to the new model of alcoholism and addiction. It is difficult to let go of our investment in fear. Even though the alternative sounds good, there is still a lingering belief that "a little fear is good." The reasoning behind this belief is that just in case God is not as good as we say He is, it may be better to hold on to a little fear. This sounds like the belief that "it is better to be safe than happy." The problem with this reasoning is that safety is paid for at the price of complete loss of peace. To believe in both a God of Love and a God of vengeance puts us in a state of conflict in which we try to live according to two completely different thought systems which are going in two different directions. Love leads to Heaven; fear leads to hell. Jesus taught, "No one can serve two masters" (Mt 6:24). Love and fear are two different masters. We have to choose which one to serve. We can't serve both. The healing of fear demands that we take responsibility for our fears and look at the foundation on which they rest. Ultimately, the healing of fear will come when we no longer see it as useful. When we can say, "Fear has never gotten us what we want," we will gladly release it. Until we totally relinquish any investment we have in fear, fear will always posses us.

Does being healed from fear mean that we will never experience it again? It means that we will not be controlled by our fears and they will gradually lose the power they have over us now. Fearful possibilities will arise in our minds, but because they are not reinforced by our self-condemnation, we will be able to deal with them appropriately. The "anxieties of the world" will always be with us, but they can no longer rob us of our peace.

Once we accept God as Good and that God's Providence can be trusted, old fears can be looked at differently and we will be able to make better choices. We now understand that we are not victims of our own fears. We have something to say about how long we will allow fear to dwell in our minds. Healing begins when we begin to take responsibility for our fears. We have a Power in us that is greater than our fears and we can call upon that Power whenever we need help.

Does being healed from fear mean that we will no longer worry about our loved ones? Somewhere along the line we picked up the notion that love and worry are the same. Actually, they contradict one another. Archbishop Fulton J. Sheen used to say that "worry is a form of atheism." When we worry about someone, we are implicitly saying that we love that person more than God does and that somehow our worry has the power to help. Worry has no power to accomplish anything and, indeed, may become an obstacle to happiness. Jesus is very clear about this in the Sermon on the Mount (Mt 6:25-35). Here he tells us "do not worry" because it cannot achieve anything and, besides, "Your Heavenly Father already knows what you need."

The reason why worry can be an obstacle to the happiness of another is that it is a form of manipulation and control which will eventually be resented. A psychological principle indicates that "dependence breeds contempt." When we worry about someone else, we presume that we know what is the best for him and we make him dependent on our desires. This form of control always backfires and produces negative results. When we worry about another, we become part of the problem and not the solution.

We obviously have concern for our loved ones. However, when the concern becomes irrational, we know that we are still in fear and that fear is the opposite of love. When we truly love someone, we respect the goodness in them and the goodness of God toward them. We want to be loving and do what is helpful. When we are healed from fear and our motivation is love, we will know exactly what to do to be truly helpful.

We must also beware of "anxious prayer" which is a contradiction in terms. On the one hand, we are saying that we are praying for someone else, but on the other hand, we don't believe that the prayer will be answered. When we become aware that we are worrying, we should ask the Holy Spirit for help. We should not get upset, but we should say to the Holy Spirit that we would rather be praying than worrying. We should acknowledge that worrying has never worked and we want to change. Then we release the person to the Holy Spirit. We let go of any personal investment we have in the outcome of our prayers and relax into the realization that we have done our part by placing this person in the hands of a loving God. Father Solanus Casey, OFM Cap., would suggest that "we thank God ahead of time" and let go of the conclusions of our prayers.

Ultimately, if fear is to be healed, there needs to be a change in our image of God. If self-condemnation is at the bottom of all our fears then the greatest symbol of judgment is God. The various forms which fear takes, namely, fear of rejection, fear of authority, fear of success, fear of sickness, etc., can all be traced back to an image of God as a conditional lover. Only when we question that image and become willing to risk a belief in God as an unconditional lover, will our fears begin to dissipate. If any teaching has been at the heart of our ministry, it is that God is an unconditional Lover. It is amazing to see the miracles that happen when people accept this belief.

Father Peter McCall

Reflections and Sharing

RISE AND BE HEALED
OF FEAR

Fear can be such a crippling emotion. Some of the synonyms for fear are: apprehension, terror, fright, panic, horror, trepidation. These all imply a painful emotion experienced when a person is confronted by threatening danger or evil. The level of fear was at an all time high recently, when the country was experiencing the war in the Persian Gulf. Iraq's leader, Saddam Hussein, had threatened to unleash poison gas and murderous chemical weapons on neighboring countries, especially Israel. The Israelis were wearing gas masks and had to seal their homes. And the world was watching this mindlessness on television in horror and disbelief. First we were told the war would last only a couple of weeks; then we were told it might go on for months. The danger of Arab terrorist attacks caused us to take precautions of every kind. Even in New York City people were buying gas masks. My fears started to rise when the media showed Arabs with a passionate hatred toward the American people. I thought with great trepidation that the war may go on for years and that the hate would be there permanently. The sad thing was, as in any war, everyone thinks they are right and God is on their side.

I began to get caught up in this way of thinking and concerned that there wasn't a solution to the problem. A gentle reminder turned my thoughts within, "Be still and know that I am God" (Ps 46:11). I am reminded by the Holy Spirit to turn once again to the Source of my life. God is Supreme. Jesus is the Prince of Peace. I turn to Jesus in prayer and gradually my peace returns. I realize there is very little I can do about the world situation other than pray for peace with justice. The best that I can do for myself and those around me is to maintain my own inner peace. Each time I am tempted to be fearful about the world situation, I turn once again to the inner presence of peace that is always waiting.

Most of my life I lived in fear and anxiety, so it is with tremendous gratitude to God that I have come this far. I probably reached the lowest ebb of my life after my fifth child was born. It was then I began to have tremendous fears. My anxiety level reached an all time high. For many months I suffered a great deal. After receiving professional help, I was encouraged to join a Bible study group. I refused to take sleeping pills and I kept the light on all night because I was afraid of the dark. I also kept the windows open, even on freezing nights, because I had a fear of being smothered. One anxious night when I could not sleep, I decided to go out to the living room and read my Bible. I opened it at random. The page fell to the Gospel of Matthew 6:19-34. I knew then, as I know now, that it was a special message for me from Jesus. Verse 27 reads, "Which of you by worrying can add a moment to his life-span?" And verse 34 reads, "Enough then of worrying about tomorrow. Let tomorrow take care of itself. Today has troubles enough of it's own." That night I felt sure Jesus was talking to me personally.

I remember thinking, "These are the very words of Jesus, himself!" I was filled with awe that he cared about me so intimately. From that night on my night terrors ceased, my fears lessened and my level of trust in his care for me was increased. On another night Jesus revealed to me that his light, which is the light of the world, is present even in the darkness, and I lost my fear of the dark.

As I began to develop my spiritual life, I fashioned the habit of rising early in the morning to start my day in prayer. One such morning as I was in deep prayer, I heard the inner voice of the Holy Spirit speak to me. His words were, "Fear will no longer have power over you." I understood this to mean that even though I would still be tempted to become fearful, it would be defused by the power of the Holy Spirit. Another time, I heard the same message only the word evil was substituted for the word fear, "Evil will no longer have power over you." I have had many fears since then and I have been overcome by evil many times, yet to my surprise and relief they have always proved to be unfounded.

The chapel where we hold our Tuesday noon healing services is not in the best neighborhood, and one Tuesday, when I pulled up in my car I noticed a man shouting at a woman, who was holding a baby. The woman was very young and she was crying. The man had her backed up against the monastery wall and kept shouting at her. I stayed in my car and began to pray. In the meantime, a group of elderly people standing across the street watched, looking alarmed. I prayed that a police car would suddenly and miraculously appear. But none did. I thought I should run past the couple, into the church, and get Father Peter to come out and rescue the woman and the baby. This seemed to be my only option. Meanwhile, the man became more agitated and I was afraid he was going to strike the woman. I cautiously got out of my car and began to walk past them, when suddenly I stopped dead in my tracks and turned to the man and said in a very bold and authoritative voice, "Leave that woman and baby alone, you are abusing them!" Much to my surprise the man turned to me and said, "What?" I repeated my message, "Leave that woman and baby alone, you are abusing them!" He looked at me long and hard, turned to the baby, and with a Cheshire Cat smile, patted the baby on top of the head, said something to the woman quietly, and left in his car. I began shaking like a leaf and after seeing that the woman and child were okay and offering them sanctuary in the chapel, I went inside and told Father Peter. I realize in hindsight that I was using the authority of Jesus and while I was under that authority there was no need to fear.

Father Peter points out that the very thing we fear can come upon us. We unconsciously set ourselves up for conditions that can create what we fear. I had prayed with a woman who had a mastectomy. Her mother had also had one. Before she developed breast cancer, this woman had been obsessed with the fear of it. She spent years trying to ensure herself against disease by taking extra precautions on a physical level. She thought Yoga and exercise classes would prevent it. She tried watching her diet — all out of fear of getting cancer. When she did get cancer, she was devastated. During our prayer sessions, she began to realize how her fear might have been a contributing factor. Our minds are extremely powerful and they can work for or against us. This woman's motivation for taking good care of herself physically originated from the fear of getting cancer, not from healthy self-caring. It is my personal belief that the negative emotions such as: anger, guilt, fear and grief can be the groundwork for the seeds of cancer and other life-threatening illnesses.

I have limited knowledge of medicine. At times I have felt I would be a better instrument of God's healing power if I had more medical knowledge. However, when Jesus wants me to know something he will allow me to experience it personally so that I will learn it and not forget. The chapel at Blessed Sacrament Monastery is holy ground for me. I have spent many hours there before the exposed Blessed Sacrament in prayer. The Sisters of the Blessed Sacrament are an order of nuns who devote their lives to adoring Jesus in the Blessed Sacrament. Their motto is, "To adore for those who do not." The highlight of their spiritual year is the observance of Holy Thursday, the celebration of the Lord's Supper, just before Easter Sunday.

About five years ago, I attended this Mass. At daily Mass the sisters sing like angels. This particular day, they seemed to be singing with the Heavenly Choirs themselves. I became completely absorbed in the beauty of the music. As the voices and the melodies blended, my soul soared to great heights. I was enraptured by the sounds and the beauty of the moment. Gradually, I became aware that I was being lifted outside of myself as though I were a spectator to myself. I became acutely aware of the atoms and cells that make up my body; I saw them as energy and that my cells had a mind and an intelligence of their own. I saw them as a consistent flow of energy moving with light. They were, in fact, dancing. I saw that they were responding to what I was feeling in my mind. The sheer delight of the beautiful spiritual music made me ecstatically happy. My body and soul felt at one with God and the cells in my body were responding in joyous celebration also.

When I returned to earth again I was in awe of what happened. I couldn't wait to tell Father Peter. In my naivete, I assumed this was a new revelation. When I told him, he informed me that this was not a new understanding. It was something I needed to learn for myself and I will never forget it. I pondered over this revelation. I reasoned that if indeed the cells in the body responded to or were stimulated by our responses to what was going on outside of us, what happens when we are in a negative frame of mind? What happens if we are living in a constant state of fear or terror? What happens to the cells in our body when we are living in a violent atmosphere? No wonder so many people we know who live in alcoholic families develop illnesses.

It is common for women to stay in unhealthy marriages out of fear. Fears come in many forms. Many of the women we have prayed with have fears of being alone, of abandonment, of homelessness and the list goes on. Many have stress-related symptoms and life-threatening illnesses, ranging from stomach distress and migraine headaches to various forms of arthritis and cancer. When my marriage fell apart, I was extremely fearful of the future. Thank God for God, He has seen me through every fear and has brought me peace. I believe we owe it to ourselves to surround ourselves in peace. I think it is a sign of healthy self-caring when we can find ways to attain this. It takes me less energy to live this way than it did when I was living in a stressful marriage.

In 1989, I received a book entitled Quantum Healing *(Bantam Books, 1989) by Dr. Deepak Chopra, a respected New England endocrinologist. I was delighted to learn that he believed in exactly what I had experienced at Blessed Sacrament Chapel on Holy Thursday three years earlier. The inside cover of his book reads:*

> Dr. Chopra shows that modern medical discoveries are beginning to verify what the Vedic sages intuited: that the human body is controlled by a 'network of intelligence' that determines whether we are sick or well, in tune with nature or out of touch with it. Not a superficial psychological state, this intelligence lies deep

enough to change the basic patterns that design our physiology - with the potential to defeat cancer, heart disease, and even aging itself!

I was amazed to find Dr. Chopra entitled one chapter "The Body Has A Mind Of Its Own." In this chapter he writes, "If a patient could promote the healing process from within, that would be the cure from cancer. Healing episodes come about when a radical shift takes place inside, removing fear and doubt at the same time it removes the disease."

Removing fear and doubt is not as easy as it seems. It is a lifelong work of being vigilant over our minds. If we want to be healed and desire to stay healthy, we must be committed to the inner life of the Spirit. My spiritual commitment lies in developing a deeper relationship with Jesus, who is my Lord and Savior. Each soul must look to it's own Higher Power for guidance. For me, it lies in that still quiet place within. I find daily meditation and centering prayer to be an integral must for my trust level to increase and to allow my fears to decrease. John the Baptist said, "He must increase while I must decrease" (Jn 3:30).

About a year ago, I awoke in the middle of the night; I tossed and turned and then decided to make better use of my time. I went to my prayer room and sat in silence. Almost immediately, I fell into a deep contemplative state. I felt the Holy Spirit urging me to go beyond what I was then experiencing. I was being urged gently to go beyond anything I had ever experienced before. I began to get in touch with fear which I translated as fear of the unknown. Again, the prompting was not to allow the fear to stop me, but to stay with it and go beyond. I began to feel myself drifting as in space. Soon enormous waves of light came. It was like an ocean. The waves of light were swirling in a circular motion and I seemed to be entering into the center of a brilliant white light. This light was pure and bright, yet I felt no fear in this presence. At that moment, I heard the words, "In this Light will you find beauty, truth and freedom from fear." I began to drift back and the white light faded away. If I had allowed my fear of the unknown to stop me, I would never have known such wonderful peace. I suppose one could say that fear is prevalent when we feel the absence of God. The awareness of the Presence of God restores us to peace.

I was in the kitchen the day before Thanksgiving. My little granddaughter, Jessica, who was three and one-half, was recovering from a bad cold. She came into the kitchen sadly and looking up into my face with searching eyes, said, "Maura, (my grandchildren call me Maura), I miss God. . . where is God?" I was rather startled and unprepared, and I said, "What did you say?" Her response was steady, "I miss God. . .where is God?" As I looked into her face, I felt sadness and concern for her. "Jessica," I said, "what makes you feel this way?" "Well, I can't see God. Why can't I see Him?", she asked. In the back of my mind, I was busy praying and asking God for guidance. My first reaction was to try to explain the unexplainable. Of course, I wanted God to appear right then and there and make everything all right again for Jessica. I made an attempt, "Well, Jessica, no one can see God because God is invisible, God is a Spirit, but we can feel God if we want to because God is everywhere." In the meantime, I was asking the Holy Spirit for help. I said, "Would you like to feel God?" Jessica was looking full in my eyes and with all the earnestness of a little child nodded, yes. I knelt down beside her in the kitchen and placed my hand on her little chest. I asked her to close her eyes. I silently prayed that she would feel God somehow. A moment passed in holy silence. She opened her eyes and there was a brightness there. I asked her if she felt God and she nodded, yes, again. With the spontaneity of a child, she started to skip off rather happily, and as she started, she said, "God talks to us too." I called to her, "Jessica, come back here, did God speak to you?" She turned around and said, "Yes, He did". "Well, what did He say?", I asked. She replied as she bounded off, "He told me, 'You are my Precious Child'".

I am sure theologians would be able to explain why Jessica missed God so much. I have a simple explanation. Jessica couldn't have missed God unless she already knew Him. I also wondered if Jessica's illness contributed to her forgetting God or whether her forgetting Him brought the illness. The fact was, she was unhappy and insecure about the separation she felt. At some level the memory of God lies with all of us. We simply forget and need to be reminded. Jessica and I joined together and reminded each other that there is nothing to fear. God is always there, ready and waiting for us.

I love you,
Maryanne Lacy

Let Us Pray:

Father, in Jesus' name, I acknowledge that no evil can come against me. May your light shine in the darkness of my fears. I believe that I am under the power and authority of the Name of Jesus. Therefore, I am safe and free from all danger. I am sustained and supported with the help of Heaven itself. Angels have been assigned to watch over and protect me all the days of my life. I am reminded that the Perfect Love of Jesus casts out all fear. The Psalms tell me, "The Lord is my light and my salvation; whom should I fear? The Lord is my life's refuge; of whom should I be afraid?" In confidence and with trust, I believe the Lord will give me the courage just when I need it. I take comfort in knowing that the Lord is my helper and my protection. The Lord is my refuge and my fortress, my God in whom I trust. How great is your goodness, oh God. You are ever present to me. You have never abandoned me. You are always with me. I have nothing to fear for I place my trust in knowing that you are watching over me. I offer you my thanksgiving with praise and adoration all the days of my life. Amen.

Chapter 6

RISE AND BE HEALED OF RELIGIOUS ADDICTION AND ABUSE

> *"Let us, then, be children no longer, tossed here and there . . . Rather, let us profess the truth in love and grow to the full maturity of Christ the head"* *(Ephesians 4:14 & 15).*

It is interesting to see what has happened in the past five years in the healing ministry. Just the other day I went to one of the largest Catholic book stores in New York State, the Graymoor Book Shop, Graymoor, NY. I had not been there for a couple of years. The last time I was there, the first section of books and tapes which caught my eyes when I walked into the shop was material related to the Charismatic Renewal. These were the popular books at that time. Now, that first section is filled with books and tapes about recovery from addictions and abuse. There has certainly been a change of consciousness.

We have become increasingly aware of the widespread effects of the dysfunctional family and the destructiveness of addictions and co-addictions on our society. We are also becoming aware that behavior we called "holy" and "pious" a few years ago was not what it seemed to be. We now know that any behavior that is compulsive and obsessive is an addiction, intended to deny what is really going on inside of us. It became evident that not even religion was excluded from the possibility of becoming an addiction. As people began to tell their stories about life in dysfunctional families, it became clear that many of us were religiously abused as children, but because it was hidden under the name of God and the Bible, we didn't realize it was abuse.

Once it is understood that religion can be addictive, we can see how it can be used to justify such irrational behavior as discrimination, hatred, wars, and social injustices. It explains how an Adolph Hitler could tell the world, "Never doubt that God is on my side." Religion becomes a perfect instrument to control and manipulate people because the highest authority possible is called upon to justify it.

Understanding that religion can be addictive also explains how an apparent conversion to God might be nothing more than a transference from one addictive form of behavior to another with no real healing taking place. This is called "cross-addiction." An individual may "cross-addict" to religion because it is more acceptable socially, but still not be healed of the addictive personality which is the heart of the problem. Often people who have "found God" begin to preach condemnation to the "Godless" while still maintaining an addiction to sex. There has not been any authentic "spiritual awakening" in such cases, only a movement back and forth between addictions.

When Jesus called the Pharisees "hypocrites," he could have just as accurately called them, "religious addicts" and "religious abusers." he Pharisees "tied up heavy burdens, hard to carry, and laid them on the shoulders of others" (Mt 23:4). This is what religious abuse is all about. Jesus called the Pharisees, "blind guides, you strain out the gnat and swallow the camel" (Mt 23:24). This is a perfect example of denial which is so typical of the addict. In Jesus' parable of the Pharisee and the Publican going up to the temple to pray (Lk 18:9-14), we see that the Pharisees saw the Publican's value and worth as a person in his external observance of the law. He got "high" on his belief that he was better than the Publican. Religion had become his "drug of choice." He was addicted to his own righteousness.

Religious addiction may take a different form than other addictions, but the underlying content is the same. When we examine the needs and motivations of the religious addict, they are similar to all addictive behavior. There are basically four characteristics of an addiction: denial, obsession, compulsiveness, and grandiosity. When we look at the religious addict, we can see all these characteristics but in a different form.

Addictions are used as smoke screens and distractions so that we don't have to look within to see what is really bothering us. Religious addicts maintain an "either/or" way of thinking which excludes the middle ground of truth. They insist on their interpretation of the Bible, and any other possibilities are ruled out. They have their "pet scriptures" which they use to resolve the most complex problems with ease. They see everything as either "black or white," and interpret any questioning about their conclusions as a personal attack. They see people as either for them or against them. They insist that everything be interpreted their way or else it deserves condemnation. If we come from a dysfunctional family, we recognize this way of thinking immediately.

All addicts are obsessed by their addiction. It occupies their minds in such a way that their whole lifestyle centers around it. This is seen in the fanaticism of the religious addict. Anything other than religion has no value. They abandon personal responsibilities toward family, friends, and finances in the name of religion. They get so involved in causes and crusades that they neglect their primary obligations. They have lost all balance in their lives because religion is the only thing that matters. In this regard there is no difference between the religious addict and the alcoholic. Only the "drug of choice" differs.

Addicts don't do what they want to do. They do what they need to do. Their lives are regimented around their addiction and options become fewer and fewer. Things have to be done the same way all the time. They are driven by rituals no matter how irrational they may have become. Religious addicts are compelled to perform certain practices out of fear of condemnation. They are "perfectionists" who demand perfection of themselves and others. They are fearful about whether their actions are pleasing to God or not. They have a strong belief in sacrifice and usually practice severe penances because of low-esteem for their bodies. Such compulsiveness is similar to the sex addicts who are just as much concerned with the rituals surrounding their addiction as they are with the pleasure they derive from their behavior. We do not have space in this book to speak about sex addiction; however, we should comment here that authorities in the field of addiction see a relationship between sex addiction and religion addiction. This may explain why many religious people also have difficulty in the area of sex.

All addictions end in isolation with the fantasy that the addict is right and the rest of the world is wrong. Addicts become judgmental and issue pronouncements of condemnation on all people. With an arrogance that only an addictive mind can justify, entire segments of humanity are judged and found guilty. Religious addicts show the same grandiosity by condemning entire world religions that don't agree with theirs. They rule out entire areas of science because they do not support their view of the Bible. They become "heresy hunters" who are always on the lookout for new errors so that they can expose them and blot them out. They have "delusions of grandeur" in which they see themselves as the guardians of truth. This type of behavior is no different from the alcoholic who projects blame for his or her situation on everyone but himself or herself. Addicts need scapegoats to justify their behavior and religious addicts are no different. They need an "enemy" outside themselves on whom they can project condemnation so they won't have to face the self-condemnation within themselves. The "holy wars" which we are experiencing in our day are nothing more than religious addictions brought to a logical conclusion.

Religious addicts become religious abusers. They inflict their extreme beliefs onto others in such a way that shame, fear and resentment result. Just as sexual abuse shames those at whom it is directed, religious abuse can disfigure a personality with guilt, fear and scrupulosity. I know a father who demands that his entire family recite the rosary every night together. If one of the children makes a mistake with words, his or her hands are slapped and the entire family has to recite the rosary all over again. They must stay there until the rosary is recited perfectly. This father is a religious addict and is abusing his family. Instances of religious abuse do not have to be as flagrant as the one just discussed. An elderly nun recently told me that when she was a little girl, her mother told her, "When girls whistle, the Mother of God cries." Any time God or the saints are used to perpetuate a custom that has nothing to do with God, that's religious abuse. Telling a child that "God is going to get you," just because he or she was disruptive and behaving like a child, is religious abuse.

John Bradshaw tells the story that when he was in the fifth grade in a Catholic elementary school, a nun brought in a picture of a diseased lung and said, "That's what your soul looks like when you are in mortal sin." Telling fifth graders that they have committed mortal sin is religious abuse. Most of us have been religiously abused, but we didn't realize it at the time. It's only in later years when we find ourselves bound by scrupulosity or subject to panic attacks that seem to come from no where, do we begin to realize that maybe they are caused by fear engendered in us by religious abuse.

How do we begin to be healed of religious addiction and abuse? Before any healing can begin, religious addiction and abuse has to be recognized as a problem and a disease. This is not as easy as it sounds. The difficulty is that religious addicts are so taken up with their grandiosity and their "specialness" with God that they are oblivious to the fact that they have a problem. Many people who were abused by religion think of their parents as "saints" and would never think of them as addicts. Just as denial is the most primitive defense against addiction, it is especially powerful in regard to religion.

Religious addicts often have places of honor within the community and are likely to be respected by others. There is no reason for a conversion or a healing when so many things are going well for them. However, religious addiction is a defense against the truth, and like all defenses, it must gradually begin to fall apart. Either the addict will be exposed by his or her other addictions, or the pain of his or her "phoniness" will eventually lead to depression or physical sickness. There are no such things as "hidden addictions." All addictions take their toll on the addict and the pain gets so great that they cry for help.

It is often difficult for a religious addict to recognize that they have a problem because when the pain and suffering caused by their addiction begins to become conscious, they rationalize it as "a cross sent by God" which they are to endure like a true martyr. Rather than seeing their pain as a call for change or healing, they embrace it because it fits into their whole system of "specialness." These "saints" will go to their graves never realizing that their suffering came from their addiction, and not from God.

The good news is that many religious addicts have spiritual awakenings and begin to realize where their pain is coming from. This explains why Fundamentalists Anonymous is such a fast growing twelve step program for religious addicts and for those abused by religion. People in our day are beginning to recognize that religion can dysfunction an entire family. The children need the same help as children who come from an alcoholic or physically abusive home. Because of this, the healing process will be similar to what we have already said about the healing of shame, anger and fear.

We have put this chapter in our book because there are many people who deny that religion can be an addiction. The same thing can be said about sex addiction. There are people, many of them therapists, who deny that sex can be an addiction. Any type of behavior that involves denial, obsessions, compulsiveness and grandiosity, is an addiction and needs to be treated as such. The one characteristic that may apply to religious addicts more than to others is the need for open-mindedness. Most religious addicts have a very narrow perception of God and The Scriptures. There is a need to "loosen up" and to be open to the idea that truth may be bigger than they thought. The "overwhelming message of

The Scriptures" must replace narrow interpretations which distort the message and end up giving us a too-small image of God.

All authentic healing is a process, a spiritual journey which we take "one day at a time." The beautiful thing is that we don't have to wait until the end to enjoy the trip. Each day we can enjoy the serenity which freedom from addictive behavior brings. We are all invited to take this journey by a God Who says to us, "You shall know the truth, and the truth will set you free" (Jn 8:32).

Father Peter McCall

Reflections and Sharing

RISE AND BE HEALED OF RELIGIOUS ADDICTION AND ABUSE

On April 21, 1991, an article appeared on the front page of The New York Times. *The headline read, "Leaner Hamburger Undergoes Trial by Taste." The article reported a new fat-free hamburger that McDonald's had concocted, and it said, "Americans love burgers and, unfortunately, burgers are bad for the national health... McDonald's is trying to correct God's mistake." If this isn't the height of arrogance, I don't know what is! It's almost laughable. Imagine making God responsible for putting fat into hamburgers! No wonder there is so much religious abuse when God is viewed in such a demeaning way. Father Peter often says that God has been made into the biggest scapegoat in the world. If we view God in this way, no wonder there is so much lack of respect for the sacred, whether it be in God or in us. Father Peter is a great believer in healing people through explanation. Sometimes explaining to people how they might be religiously abusive or addictive can break through the ignorance associated with this subject. Again, the defense mecha-*

nism of denial has to be dealt with. Father Peter has pointed out that denial is especially stubborn where religion is concerned.

A very dear friend of mine asked me to pray for her father. He was suffering with a heart condition, but was keeping it a secret from the family, or so he thought. The reason for the secrecy, she explained, was because her dad believed that sickness is a punishment from God for sins committed. When he was a boy, his father would beat him if he even so much as caught a cold. The father's reasoning was that if his son was sick then he must have sinned against God. It was his duty as a father to help God punish this boy for his sins. As a result, her father is afraid to let anyone know he is sick. He still lives in fear and guilt. Another man, who is in recovery now, was told by his mother when he was small that little boys who display anger will go directly to hell.

One time a man called us at the House of Peace frantically day after day asking for prayers for his wife who had cancer. His wife never called us. This man was very persistent, which was not unusual, although his wife didn't seem too interested. He persuaded her to come to some of the healing services. He also convinced her to see us for a personal appointment. He was desperate to see her healed. While we were in conference with them, this man shared with us how deep his religious life was. He went to daily Mass, said the rosary many times a day, and made countless novenas. Finally, he told us in front of his wife, that he felt God was punishing her by giving her cancer. The reason, he said, was because she had not given her life to God and

129

religion the way he had. She wouldn't even go to daily Mass with him. He was pretty angry and felt justified in his beliefs. Father Peter and I were astounded, to say the least. There was no way we could change his mind. Soon after this meeting, we received the message that his wife had died. We were not at all surprised by this news. The man has never been in touch with us since.

I think there must be a great deal of arrogance associated with religious addiction. I was once told by a fundamentalist lady that the Miraculous Medal of Our Blessed Mother, which I was wearing around my neck, was worshiping false idols. I replied, "If I had a picture of my own mother in a locket around my neck, would that be considered worshiping false gods also?" So much separation and hurt is caused by this kind of self-righteous thinking.

Religious abuse can occur in Charismatic Prayer Groups when there isn't proper supervision. A woman I know was severely damaged by a prayer group leader in her parish. Veronica (name changed for protection) joined her local parish prayer group at a time when she was quite vulnerable. She was going through many changes in her life and had numerous doubts about herself. She lacked self-esteem and felt unsure about her life and who she was. She thought that the prayer group leader must be very special and anointed by God to be in her position, and as time went on Veronica became very close to her. At one point, the group leader told Veronica that she should not let just anyone cut her hair, and if she did, she would lose her power. The prayer group leader indicated that she would reveal who the right person was to do the job.

Veronica began getting anxiety attacks. Around the same time, a neighbor with whom Veronica had a disagreement, died. Her anxiety increased. Her friend, the leader, suggested that she might be under the influence of the devil and that is why she was feeling anxiety. As Veronica's anxiety continued to increase, she retreated to the safety of her home. In time, she became agoraphobic (a condition in which a person has an abnormal fear of being out in the open). The leader decided Veronica was possessed by her dead neighbor's spirit, which she thought was evil. She told Veronica she had special powers to cast out evil spirits and showed her special oils which would help do the trick. Veronica told me that this person was so convincing, she went along with it out of fear.

Veronica's husband became alarmed by Veronica's behavior and was not supportive of it in any way. Veronica began to have panic attacks, and at this point, decided to get advice from her parish priest and a nun whom she trusted. Through their loving guidance they helped her out of her confusion. Veronica began a Twelve Step Program where she started to realize how she had set herself up to be religiously abused by a religious addict. Now, six years later, she is in recovery and very much at peace with herself. For a long time she would flee from any association with the Charismatic Renewal, but now understands what happened, and that there are many loving people involved in this movement. She advises anyone to beware of

*people who focus on evil rather than on the love of God
and to be wary of prayer group leaders who tend to use
their role for power in order to control others. The religious addict tends to be egoistic and grandiose. If you
are uncomfortable with the person, follow your instincts
and seek help. Thank God Veronica was rescued.*

 *In the healing prayer ministry, a method of lay-
ing-on-of-hands, referred to as soaking prayer, is fre-
quently used. This is to allow the flow of God's loving,
healing energy to penetrate an area of disease or emotional disturbance until the problem disintegrates. We
received a phone call from a woman who had been
observing this method at one of our healing services.
When she asked if we were using therapeutic touch, we
explained that we were using soaking prayer. She said
she was relieved because she had heard from a segment
of leadership in the Charismatic movement that therapeutic touch was from the devil. And another friend of
ours, who is a registered nurse, and uses therapeutic
touch in her work, was told at a prayer meeting that
she should not do this because it was of the occult. This
nurse is a deeply committed Christian and, needless to
say, never returned to the prayer group again. I con-
sulted our friend, Sheila Levy, a nurse, and a member
of our ministry. Sheila took a course on Therapeutic
Touch with Dolores Krieger, R.N. at the New York
University School of Nursing. Sheila and all the other
students experienced this method and felt profoundly
rested and were quite surprised by the positive results.
She said its primary and essential purpose was love.
She added that the word therapeutic is defined as per-*

taining to the art of healing. Within our ministry one can only hope to be a channel for the healing power of Jesus. The laying-on-of-hands is a loving touch which could be called a therapeutic touch. However, it is always in the name of Jesus that we pray for healing.

Everyone in the world is unique and individual. No one has the right to dictate to other human beings what is right or wrong for them. Each person must decide for himself or herself in prayer and with the guidance of the Holy Spirit what method or modality of healing is best. It may be laying-on-of-hands, therapeutic touch, acupressure, acupuncture; or it may be chemotherapy, radiation, counseling, nutrition, exercise or massage. There are hundreds of different healing techniques and each person has the right to choose which direction to take.

Religious abuse comes in so many forms. It would be impossible to recount them all here. When I was young the Blessed Mother and Saints were presented to us as role models that we could not possibly live up to. This is religious abuse. I was attending Mass in Florida last winter. It was a weekday Mass and the parish school children were in attendance. During the homily, the priest asked the children to pray that they might become priests or nuns. He went on and on extolling the virtues of such vocations. He gave the distinct impression that becoming a priest or nun was the only true way one could serve God in this world. There was absolutely no mention that holiness can be attained in the laity.

Once Father Peter and I paid a visit to an eleven-year-old Hispanic boy who was in the hospital. His parents were young, spoke little English, and couldn't explain what the child's illness was. He had a great deal of pain in his legs from some mysterious malady. The pains would come and go, but at times he was in agony. We told him who we were, that Father Peter was a priest and that we were going to bless and pray for him. He looked up at Father Peter and began to cry out, "Do you think God will forgive me for all the sins I have committed?" We were startled to hear an eleven-year-old in such an anguished state of mind. Father assured him that God had already forgiven him, there was no need to fear. All the boy could say was, "Oh, Father, I hope God has forgiven me." We assured him that God had forgiven him. During the short time we spent with him, he would cry out repeatedly in pain, and ask again and again, "Do you think God has forgiven all my sins?" I can't begin to describe my astonishment and my sadness as I stood at his bedside praying for him. The thought passed through my mind that he must be punishing himself for something that he felt was too awful to reveal. A nurse came in and we had to leave. As we walked down the corridor from his room, we could only wonder who had been influencing this child to believe that God might possibly be punishing him in this way?

We have been given a tremendous responsibility as Christians to educate our children regrading an unconditionally loving God. However, looking back over the years, after I raised my children, I wonder if I made the right choice in sending them to parochial schools. I think that when a school professes to be Christian, it has a major responsibility to practice what it preaches, otherwise it is teaching hypocrisy. When discipline is attained by fear and not love, the privilege of educating children is being abused. Jesus warned against this kind of religious abuse in the Gospel of Matthew, "Their words are bold but their deeds are few. They bind up heavy loads, hard to carry, to lay on other people's shoulders, while they themselves will not lift a finger to budge them" (23:4).

All of my children have reported incidents of emotional abuse in school. One teacher terrified first graders by saying she had a whipping machine in the closet. Another threatened the class with a paddle. My daughter, Mary, thought that certain children were used as scapegoats and were humiliated in front of the class. She remembers feeling sorry for her friends, but very glad it wasn't happening to her. My daughter, Kathy, remembers how a teacher told her that she was a distraction to the boys in her class. She arranged the desks into a circle and put Kathy in the center of it as punishment. Kathy, being a sensitive child, was deeply wounded by the shame and it affected her for many years.

My other children have also shared some unpleasant parochial school experiences with me. For some, the healing is yet to come, while with others the healing has already come with the grace of understanding. Two of my daughters had the unique opportunity of working in a religious infirmary, taking care of sick and elderly nuns. There they began to see things differently. These

135

women had been hurt and disillusioned like everyone else, and my daughters were able to see them as real people. They began to realize that the nuns in school did the best they knew how at the time, and the only option for healing lies in forgiveness. All of my children believe they will be very selective in choosing schools for their own children. They will investigate the school and teachers before making a choice. And in defense of their parochial school training, they believe it did help shape their lives for good. Perhaps this is why my husband and I chose a Catholic education for our children. I only know that we thought we were doing our best at the time. I know I wanted my children to be grounded in the faith that I love so much. I have had to forgive myself countless times for making mistakes as a parent and for my own immature spirituality. I certainly ask my children their forgiveness for my ignorance. It is the role of Jesus and the work of the Holy Spirit to bring about redemption through the healing process. Trust in God's healing love brings me peace and I know He will bring order and wholeness in time to all my children.

I can honestly say that I did not learn the love of God during my own years in parochial school. I did learn to love the Mass. I especially looked forward to Benediction and it is still one of my favorite rituals for praising God.

I have come to admire the relationship Father Peter has had with God, the Father. It took me many years of inner healing before I could believe in a loving Heavenly Father. I know that all forms of abuse affect our relationship with God in one way or another. Father

Peter has always known God as an unconditionally loving Father, because he had the good fortune of having a very caring earthly father. Father Peter often gets exasperated when people say things like, "God sent cancer to my wife," or something similar. I chuckle, because he will immediately reply "Please don't talk about my Heavenly Father that way. He is not like that at all." He will acclaim the wonderful goodness of God. I think Father Peter is one of God's best public relations men. I was once told by my spiritual director that I needed to forgive God not for the things He didn't do, but for the things I thought He did. I can only credit my prayer life and deepening relationship with Jesus for leading me out of that destructive mode of thinking. Fortunately, we are in a ministry that validates and confirms Father Peter's convictions about the Goodness of God.

A few years ago, we were asked to do a healing service for a nearby veterans hospital. Both staff and patients were invited to attend. A few of the nurses we prayed with became ecstatic with joy. We were so happy to see them radiate with the love of Jesus. Soon after, a patient, a man in a hospital robe, came up to us for prayer. I remember him quite well because he seemed so sad and sick. He was a tall man and as he stood in line waiting, I recall noticing and being concerned for him. I will call him Jacob. When it was time for him to be prayed with, we asked his name and what he wanted us to pray for. He barely mentioned his name and couldn't respond, so we didn't know what we were praying for. We just laid our hands on him and prayed in silent tongues. Suddenly Jacob began to weep deeply. I suggested to Father Peter that he embrace Jacob. He did, and Jacob began to weep more and more. While we were praying over him he rested in the Spirit. He shared with us later that three times he tried to keep from falling, but couldn't resist the Holy Spirit and laid down. These are his own words: "I was weeping again, still unable to speak, but not tears of sorrow, these were tears of joy. I felt love and inner peace. The healing prayers were continued over my body until the tears stopped and I extended my arms towards God and the Holy Spirit." When Jacob was able to get up, we asked him how he felt. He could only reply, "Loved."

A few days later we received a call from the chaplain of the hospital telling us that a patient had been healed of AIDS during the healing service and that we would be hearing from him. It was Jacob, and in his testimony, he shared that he was a Viet Nam veteran and had been away from the Church for many years because of guilt and fear. He said that when Father Peter embraced him, he felt that Mother Church had welcomed him back and that a white light had entered his body just before he rested under the Power of the Holy Spirit. The next day, the doctors told him that the HIV test had come out negative. They decided to re-test in case it was false, but the results of the second test were negative again. Everyone was astounded because when he had been admitted to the hospital he was found to have a protein associated with the AIDS virus that was killing his brain cells and had been diagnosed with

AIDS. Also, he had lesions on his lungs which disappeared after the healing prayers.

All of this happened about five years ago, and as far as we know, although Jacob is still working through emotional problems, he is still physically well. Jacob told us how he tried to hide out from God and his family after returning from Viet Nam. He thought his sins were too terrible for anyone to forgive and he suffered terribly for many years. He was to discover that God is the "Hound of Heaven."

Stories like these are what make this ministry of healing so worthwhile. We want to shout and proclaim from the housetops God's Wondrous, Glorious Love.

I love you,
Maryanne Lacy

Let Us Pray:

Father, God, I have come before you to ask your pardon. I have had the tendency to see you in the same way I viewed my parents. I thought you were critical and judgmental. I thought I had to do a lot of begging and praying just to be heard. I believed that if I were not perfect I would be punished by you. Heal me, Oh Lord, of memories of oppression I felt because of religion and religious observances during the years of my childhood. I grew up thinking you were a hard taskmaster and I was deathly afraid of you. I have come to realize I had been projecting the image of my mother and father upon you.

Father, I know you have already pardoned me for you are an unconditional lover. You are incapable of holding a grievance against your children. I need to forgive myself for believing in lies about you. I ask you to send comfort to my frightened inner child who at times finds it difficult to embrace the notion of a God who loves so dearly and unconditionally. I ask your help to distinguish between outward religious observance and true spirituality. Help me to worship you in Spirit and in Truth. I need to be healed from the inside out because I grew up spiritually impoverished. This led me to temptations and sin and self-destructive tendencies. I turned to overeating, drugs, alcohol, gambling and sick relationships. I am so ashamed of the ways in which I tried to veil my pain.

I am slowly beginning to learn to love myself in healthy ways with the help of Jesus and the Holy Spirit. I am beginning to experience what it really means to be a precious Child of God with feelings of joy and peace. I am becoming more aware that you, oh, Lord, are on my side. I choose to believe that you are intimately concerned for my welfare. You are God, You are Love, there is no other! I thank you for revealing to the merest of children what you have concealed from the worldly and wise. You are unfolding to me your magnificent true nature. You are an Infinite Wellspring of loving kindness. I am slowly allowing myself to trust in and receive more of your Unconditional Love. Remove from my heart and mind any block that religion has created.

Continue to reveal to me my true spiritual nature and unlock the bars of defenses I placed around my heart and mind. I thank you for bringing to light the spiritual richness that is my inheritance as your beloved child. I thank you also for the many gifts and graces you have already bestowed on me. I had but to recognize that you are the Giver of all Goodness and you want only my highest good. Thank you, Father, Son and Holy Spirit. I will praise and extol your name forever and ever. Amen.

Chapter 7

RISE AND BE HEALED OF DEPRIVATION NEUROSIS

> *"Is it only myself and Barnabas who are forced to work for a living? What soldier in the field pays for his own rations? . . . It is written in the law of Moses, 'you shall not muzzle an ox while it treads out grain'"* *(1 Corinthians 9:6,7,8).*

One of the effects of being raised in a dysfunctional family and in an addicted society is that our basic human needs could not be met. We come into adulthood with what John Bradshaw calls, "a hole in our soul." We try to fill that hole in a variety of ways. We try alcohol, drugs, food, work, sex, and other addictions in an attempt to alleviate the sense of scarcity, but the need is insatiable and "there is never enough" to satisfy. For the sake of a name, we will call this condition "deprivation neurosis." It is a chronic state of mind in which we accept scarcity as our normal condition here on earth.

Feelings of deprivation originated when we were taught that we were defective, flawed, and that we lacked what it took to succeed and prosper. I can remember a nun, a teacher of mine in the eighth grade, who was upset at something I had done, saying to me in front of the whole class, "Peter McCall, you will never be as good as your brothers, and you will never amount to anything." When statements like that are made by authority figures to whom others look for guidance and direction, we cannot help but feel inadequate and deprived. Whenever we are shamed, we feel abandoned, alone, and separated from the very people who are supposed to fill our need for love and acceptance. Whenever guilt is used to manipulate us, the natural result is that we feel unworthy of good and we begin to miss opportunities to succeed and prosper.

Deprivation neurosis can manifest itself in many different forms. We can see it in people who constantly sabotage their good, who are accident prone, and who settle for far less than they can accomplish. It is manifested in our competitiveness when we try to prove that we are better than others so as to relieve our own sense of inadequacy. It is seen in our greed to covet possessions and power to make up for the sense of lack within. We see it in people who hoard things, who cannot throw anything away because of the fear of losing what they possess. We see it in people who are excessively frugal and who are tight-fisted in their willingness to share what they have.

A sense of deprivation can be learned early in life. Families who came through the Great Depression or who were raised in poverty often accept deprivation as a way of life. Sociologists speak about a ghetto mentality which people develop when they resign themselves to their social and economic condition. Deprivation can be a generational and ethnic problem in which a collective mass of peoples see themselves as victims of the world around them and act out this sense of deprivation by settling for mediocrity in their lives.

While most people react to deprivation by under-achieving, some people respond by over-achieving. They try to fill in their sense of scarcity with "workaholism," gathering possessions, power, and prestige. This works for a while, but because their success is nothing more than a defense against their feelings of inadequacy, it eventually falls apart. We call this a mid-life crisis. We thought that we could alleviate the pain of deprivation by achieving certain financial stability, status, or fame. However, in a moment of truth, we realize that the whole thing was a hoax and our inner emptiness begins to reveal itself. We feel cheated, disillusioned, and betrayed. Actually, all that was happening was that we were acting out our deprivation neurosis. We fell into the trap which says that external success can satisfy an inner hunger.

Some people respond to deprivation neurosis with the attitude "if you can't beat it, join it." These are the people who glorify poverty and spiritualize it as the highest path to God. It may be true that some people can decide that a voluntary life of poverty and simplicity is beneficial for them as a path to God. However, to spiritualize poverty and claim that

God loves the poor more than the rich is presumptuous and theologically false. For most people poverty does not bring them closer to God, but has the opposite effect — jealousy, resentment, and social violence. My experience teaches me that only those who know God as an abundant Giver of all good things are capable of embracing a life of voluntary poverty. The best example of this is Saint Francis of Assisi. Because he was born into wealth and abundance, he was in a position to put it aside without resentment and choose what he saw as a better way to God. However, he never suffered from deprivation neurosis because he saw God as an abundant Father who would take care of all his needs. He could embrace poverty as a way of life because he did not see himself as a victim of the world around him. Those who suffer from deprivation neurosis blame God for their condition and are not happy in their poverty.

In our healing ministry, we can see where deprivation neurosis blocks the healing power of Jesus Christ. People come for healing prayer, but because of their sense of unworthiness and their narrow image of God, set themselves up not to be healed. They ask for healing, but in a very apologetic manner. At some level, they really don't believe that God would heal them because they think His will for them is suffering and deprivation. This belief did not originate with them, but was passed down from generation to generation by theologians and spiritual writers who taught that God wants us to suffer in this life in order to be happy with Him forever in the next. It is this kind of thinking that prompted

146

Karl Marx to call religion "the opium of the people." When people believe that suffering is God's will and that they should be content with their lot here on earth, they become "drugged" to any urge for the improvement of their condition. This guarantees that the status quo will be maintained. The mind that does not seek for something better than it already has cannot be healed. Many people who ask for healing really don't want it because they are not convinced that God is offering them a better way than the way they have already chosen.

The purpose of any healing ministry is to improve our way of life and bring us inner peace. Jesus summed up his ministry with the words, "I have come that they may have life and have it more abundantly" (Jn 10:10). Saint Ireaneus tells us, "The glory of God is man (all of us) fully alive." Unless we begin to question the idea that suffering and deprivation are God's will, we will be constantly vacillating between accepting our highest good and sabotaging it in the name of humility. We must take literally the words of Jesus, "My Father is glorified that you bear much fruit" (Jn 15:8). We must begin to believe that God is an abundant Father and that His will for us is prosperity, health, and wholeness.

The healing of deprivation neurosis usually begins when we first become aware of our resistance to it. There is a part of us that does not want to be happy and prosperous. This part of us is our "false-self" which is based on beliefs and assumptions diametrically opposed to healing. This is "self-denial" in the truest sense of the word. When Jesus told us we must deny ourselves (Mt 16:24), he was not talking about our "true-selves," — the part of us created by God. He was talking about our "false-selves," that is, that part of us we made which is opposed to God and our highest good. A true asceticism is reflected by the words of Jesus, "Unless a grain of wheat falls into the ground and dies, it remains just a grain of wheat. But if it dies, it produces much fruit" (Jn 12:24). We must search for and expose those negative beliefs and assumptions which form the foundation of our "false-selves" before we can affirm the truth about ourselves. We must look at our misconceptions, admit that we believe in them, and ask ourselves if we want to maintain them or not.

Many beliefs form the foundation of deprivation neurosis. We did not invent these beliefs, nor did our parents, nor their parents. These beliefs are multi-generational and have been passed down through the ages. Our beliefs are as old as the human race itself. They are part and parcel of our human inheritance. Humanity suffers from deprivation because these beliefs have rarely been challenged.

The first belief centers around victimization. Maintaining that we are victims of the world around us guarantees that we will be deprived all our lives. If we see ourselves as victims we will not only blame others for our lack of prosperity, but we will also resign ourselves to the assumption that there is nothing we can do about it. What makes this belief so powerful is that we can find a great number of witnesses to support it.

The world we live in wants to see victims and victimizers. The media is constantly telling us about

148

"poor victims" and "cruel victimizers." If we want to be healed, we cannot go along with a thought system that glorifies victimization. The only hope that such a system offers is that we can "make the best of a bad situation." An example of this is the whole psycho-analytic system of Sigmund Freud. Despite all his insights into personality development, he remained a pessimist in regard to human happiness. This was because he was trying to heal a thought system by remaining in that system. This cannot be done. If we want to be healed, we have to go outside the system that made us sick and see the world from a totally different point of view.

Jesus' thought system goes beyond the system of this world and teaches us that we have a power within us that is greater than any power the world offers. This is the good news as taught by Jesus Christ. The Power of the Holy Spirit translates the world we see into a totally different reality. The Holy Spirit teaches that we are responsible for how we feel because we don't see facts, but only our interpreta-tion of facts. For this reason we can change our interpretation from victimization to what makes us victors. We obviously can't do this alone, but with the Holy Spirit's help, we can do it.

Another belief that maintains deprivation is that we have to compete for what we get. Competi-tion is glorified in an addicted society and we can find plenty of witnesses who will tell us that attack is justified. We hear expressions like, "It's a dog-eat-dog world," or, "Do it to another before he/she does it to you." Competition is based on the idea that our prosperity is achieved at the expense of another. It says, "I am increased when another is decreased." The whole philosophy of the system is "kill or be killed." The weakness of this system should be seen in the many complex safeguards we have developed to protect what we possess. Once we believe that we have to fight for what we get, we also have to fear that someone else will come along and take it away.

True prosperity is the fruit of sharing, not attacking. We do not increase at the expense of someone else. We prosper when we join with others. The thought system of the world says that we are prosperous when we have more money than someone else. An example of this is a bumper sticker that says, "The one who dies with the most toys, wins." True prosperity has nothing to do with "things." It has to do with our attitude toward "things." There is an expression, "Happiness is not having what we want, but wanting what we have." Authentic prosperity is beyond possessions. It is an attitude which suggests that what we have is not worth having unless we share it.

Another belief that maintains deprivation is that success and prosperity are all a matter of luck — "Success is a matter of luck; ask any failure." We see this today in the widespread addiction to gambling. We don't have space in this book to talk about the specific addiction to gambling, but we are becoming increasingly aware of just how insidious this addiction is in our society. The highly publicized story of baseball star Pete Rose shows that this addiction is not limited to those who are poor and who hope to get rich quickly. We know how many people have an investment in luck by the success of state lotteries and legalized gambling casinos. There are many people in our addicted society who believe that "Lady Luck" holds the strings to their happiness.

We hear many stories about families which are torn apart by gambling. What keeps the belief in luck alive is the assumption that some people are more "special" than others. We all like to read about the poor laborer who played one ticket in the Lotto game and became an instant millionaire. We fantasize that someday this will happen to us and in a magical moment we will be transformed from a miserable creature into someone who lives "happily ever after." However, we forget that true prosperity can never be given to us by another. The tragic lives of millionaires like Howard Hughes should tell us that riches are more of the spiritual world than the material world. Mother Theresa of Calcutta may have few possessions, but no one would doubt her wealth of spirit. She may have a vow of poverty, but she is lacking in nothing. She does not suffer from deprivation neurosis.

Once we let go of the beliefs that keep us deprived, we can grow into the truths that will truly set us free to experience authentic prosperity. Once we understand that the cause of deprivation is in our mind, we see that the foundation of our abundant living is also there. We are first fulfilled in our inner life which now expresses itself in our outer world. Those who have been healed of deprivation neurosis have a new vision in which they see the things of this world differently. Prosperity is an attitude based on solid principles which we will now discuss.

Authentic prosperity is based on the belief that God is an abundant Giver and that His Will for us is always good. Abundant life is our inheritance as children of God and we become co-creators with God in our quest for the highest good. We believe that God has already given us all we need for an abundant life and that He supports us as we draw this good to ourselves. God's creation is governed by laws. By putting ourselves in alignment with those laws, good comes to us. Saint Paul expressed this principle when he wrote, "Indeed, everything is ordered for your benefit so that grace bestowed in abundance may bring greater glory to God" (2 Cor 4:15).

Once we accept that God has given us dominion over this earth and that He has ordered all things for our benefit, our success or failure in taking advantage of these laws becomes our personal responsibility. We participate with God for our highest good. There is a German expression, "God feeds the birds of the air, but he does not throw the food into their nests."

However, even our cooperation with God for our own good is God's gift to us. We cannot take even our first steps toward our good by our own power. We need to be empowered by a Higher Power that is within us, but not our own. We must first become aware of our own powerlessness before we can claim and exercise this Higher Power. Jesus tells us, "You will receive power when the Holy Spirit comes upon you" (Acts 1:8).

Another basic principle of abundant life is that giving and receiving are the same. What this means is that we must keep the flow of energy going by not only accepting good into our lives, but by giving it back to others. An example of this is the ancient custom of tithing. It has been demonstrated through the ages that there is a correlation between giving and receiving. In the business world it is expressed by the maxim, "You must spend money to make money." In the spiritual world it is expressed best by Jesus, "Give and gifts will be given to you; a good measure, packed together, shaken down, and overflowing will be poured into your lap. For the measure with which you measure will in turn be measured out to you" (Lk 6:38). Authentic prosperity comes from giving and receiving with joy. We should pay all our bills with thanksgiving and appreciation. We follow these principles at the House of Peace. We tithe to what we see as worthy causes and share our income with those in need. We can truly say that all our needs have been met and that we have been well provided for during these years.

We open ourselves up to abundant living by faith which expresses itself in expectation and anticipation of good. We have already seen that faith is always powerful. When we firmly believe that we are worthy of good, not by our merits, but by creation, we set ourselves up for good and draw it to ourselves. This faith becomes manifest in our praise and thanksgiving to God. We can't sincerely praise God if we believe that He would withhold any good from us or that He would take away the good we already have. Our praise simply affirms our belief in a God who is Good. Abundance comes to us when we are ready for it, and we reveal our readiness by acknowledging the Source of our good through praise and thanksgiving.

Finally, abundant life flows through us when we realize that our greatest joy in this world is doing the Will of God. Only in God is abundant life possible because as the Psalmist says, "Only in God is my soul at rest" (Ps 62:1). The only real sign of authentic prosperity is inner peace. This peace comes when we know that our will and God's Will are the same and there is no conflict between us. The truly rich are those who have let go of all barriers to the awareness of God's love and who are at home with God even in this world.

We do not have to wait for Heaven. Saint Theresa of Avila tells us "It's Heaven all the way to Heaven." Jesus tells us, "The Kingdom of God is already in your midst" (Lk 17:21). Those who enter more deeply into the Kingdom of God here on earth are healed from deprivation neurosis and are enjoying the wealth of the Kingdom right now.

Father Peter McCall

Reflections and Sharing

RISE AND BE HEALED OF DEPRIVATION NEUROSIS

It seems to me from what Father Peter has written that this world, certainly the world I am involved in, is based on scarcity. I'm always running out of paper towels, toilet tissue, paper napkins and tissues. Even though wealthy people can afford to ensure that they will have a steady supply of things, the simple fact is that they will always run low and have to be replaced. The scarcity principle that boggles me the most is time and sleep. I have heard others say, and I certainly agree, that there just aren't enough hours in a day. We need a 36-hour day! I'm forever trying to catch up on my sleep. Just when I feel I've gotten enough rest, another day comes and I have to replenish once again. Everything in this world either runs out, gives out, or wears out sooner or later. I saved up enough money a few years ago to buy some lovely living room furniture. It's already showing signs of wear and is faded in spots. No wonder Jesus admonishes us in Matthew "Do not lay up for yourselves earthly treasure. Moths and rust corrode; thieves break in and steal. Make it your practice instead to store up heavenly treasure, which neither moths nor rust corrode nor thieves break in and steal"

(6:19). Jesus tells many parables about riches and money in the Gospels. I have come to the conclusion that the only thing Jesus is telling us is not to make anything in this world too important. Nothing in this world is lasting.

Early in my spiritual journey, I loved to read the lives of the Saints. One particular Saint who impressed me greatly was St. John Vianney, better known as the Cure of Ars, (France, 1786-1859). He was a simple man, a priest and confessor. People would travel from all over Europe to the country village of Ars to seek him out for his wise counsel. He was highly regarded and known for his devout holiness. Sometimes his housekeeper would come to him in alarm to inform him that there was no food, and the dough for baking bread was down to the last bit. He would bless the dough and tell her to bake it. There was always a multiplication of bread and they never ran out.

In 1978 I attended the New England Charismatic Conference in Rhode Island where I heard Father Rick Thomas, a Jesuit, speak. He related how he and a small group of people were inspired to go to the garbage dumps of Tijuana, Mexico to help the poorest of the poor. The first Thanksgiving Day, when they were preparing the usual turkey dinner for themselves, there was a knock at the door and it was someone asking for food. Soon, another knock, and for the rest of that day there was a steady stream of visitors asking for food. Father Rick told us that they fed hundreds of people from the little they had. They did not run out of food and, in fact, had enough left over to distribute to the local orphan-

age. From then on whatever food they had on hand, when distributed to the poor, would not run out until the last person of that day was fed.

I can remember one morning when I was going to make lunch for my five children, I realized I had only one small can of tuna fish in the cabinet and nothing else nutritious enough. I had to make six sandwiches because my son always took two. I made the tuna fish salad and I prayed that there would be more than enough. To my amazement, I made six sandwiches without scrimping. Another evening I made a small roast for our usual family of five children and two adults, and it would have been just enough for us. Just before we were about to eat, we had unexpected visitors, friends of ours who happened to be passing through the area. Out of courtesy I invited them to stay for dinner and they accepted. I was nervous, wondering if there would be enough to go around. Again, I prayed and asked that there would be more than enough food. You guessed it! There were leftovers. Multiplication never happened whenever I had enough food. I tried it and it didn't work. The miracle occurred when there was an apparent scarcity.

Although by now I know in the Kingdom of God there is no such word as scarcity, it is interesting to note that the four Gospels: Matthew 14:7, 15:32; Mark 6:35; Luke 9:12; and John 6:5, record the miraculous multiplication of the loaves and fishes by Jesus. In the Gospel of John, Jesus tells us, "I solemnly assure you, the one who has faith in me will do the works I do and greater far than these. Why? Because I go to the Father

157

*and whatever you ask the Father in my name I will do"
(14:12). Many people I know think that asking God
for material things or money is wrong. But, Jesus tells
us numerous times to ask. "Anything you ask in my
Name I will do" (Jn 14:14). There is a lesson in humility in asking and receiving. I think people deprive
themselves because they neglect to ask. I have walked
this walk of faith long enough to know that it's true.*

*One of the first principles for overcoming scarcity
thinking is developing an attitude of gratitude regardless of our circumstances. I discovered this quite by
accident while I was spending a summer day at a
friend's vacation home. We were remarking that there
seemed to be enough fish in the oceans of the world to
feed all the hungry people. I remember thanking God
with my friend for the abundance of fish in the ocean.
About an hour later, as we walked along, a man approached us; he had caught an enormous fish but
didn't need it. He wanted to know if one of us could
use it. I had a family to feed and was quite grateful for
the fish. Another time, a friend of mine was concerned
about the drought we were experiencing. She expressed
fear about it and said that she had stopped taking
showers and was using water sparingly. Instinctively,
I felt that even though we should not waste water, we
should also not buy into the system of fear about it and
I told her my feeling. I thanked God for the abundance
of rain. I was relieved and happy to be affirmed when
very soon afterward it rained for a month.*

*Another important principle in the healing of de-
privation neurosis is to become more aware of the words*

*we speak. Words have power and we must never under-
estimate the power of our minds. Words have power
because they reflect thoughts. Negative words have
power to create negative happenings. Positive thoughts
and words have power to draw good to us. Some of the
limiting ideas that I heard from some people are:
"There's never enough money... I can't afford that...
There's a recession, we'd better cut back... Money
doesn't grow on trees... Money is the root of all evil...
I never have enough money to pay my bills." I have
come to believe that this mentality is closely connected
with a belief in victimization and loss of self-worth. I
suppose I could say that I am still in recovery regarding
this subject and its belief system. The hurt runs very
deep and in writing this chapter I began to uncover the
depth and extent of the woundedness that lies within.
My mother died when I was two years old. My brother,
who was only nine months old, was the youngest of six
children. I was next to the youngest and so was deprived
very early of the basic nurturing that I needed. My
family was recovering from the Depression Era, hence,
I started out with a sense of loss and neediness. In my
earliest memories I see myself as a delightful child.
Despite the tragedy in my life, I had a great deal of joy.
I remember that people used to love to listen to me talk
and thoroughly enjoyed themselves. However, in time,
that light was extinguished for a long time. It took
about twenty years to recover that lost child.*

*I was raised in a rather ascetic way. Not that my
family was poor. My father made a fair salary, but he
seemed to always be in debt. He also remarried and*

*added three more children to the family. We were raised
in a system and a time when children were considered
far less important than adults. Our needs or wants were
not even considered. We received an authoritarian and
domineering upbringing from the adults in our house.
We lived a fearful and oppressive existence. We were
ordered what to think, what to say, what to wear, what
to eat, and where to go well into our grown-up years.
We paid a harsh price when we disobeyed. We learned
self- denial and forbearance because this was the only
way to survive. It was not uncommon for one of us to
be sent to the bakery to buy delicious pastries for the
adults to enjoy after the children had gone to bed. To
this day, I still enjoy looking at pastries but refrain from
eating them.*

*The austerity of my childhood shaped my character
and my life during the years I was married. I entered
into marriage with the mentality that I deserved very
little - not that I was conscious of it. I was quite fortu-
nate, so I thought, just to have a husband and a home
to call my own. Until the time of my divorce, twenty-five
years later, I didn't even know what my husband's
salary was. I thought I had no rights since he earned
the money and I was just the housewife who stayed home
and took care of the children. I never had spending
money until I took a part time job when the youngest of
my five children started school. It wasn't until I had a
spiritual enlightenment and began to experience God's
unconditional love that I would begin to see my true
worth. Ironically, it was during the painful years of*

separation and finally divorce that I discovered more of God's abundance and goodness.

Father Peter loves the quote that originated in AlAnon, "As children we might have been victims, but as adults we are volunteers." When it dawned on me in therapy how I had set up my life to be a victim and a martyr, I was sick. With help I was able to work through forgiving myself for the sick role I had played. In time I came to understand that no one was to blame. If blame is laid, it must be put on the dysfunctional system and the addictive society in which we live. Having come through all this, I still had to deal with my fears regarding money and whether I could provide for myself. At this time, I was in full time ministry with the House of Peace. Father Peter and I had founded the healing center, but we did not charge for our services, nor do we now. We depend totally on free will offerings from people who feel led by the Holy Spirit to help us. (Father Peter would say to me that he took the vow of poverty as a Capuchin Franciscan, but that I live it. By this he meant that through his Order he was well taken care of; however, I had no means of support.) My youngest daughter, who is a single parent, and I were raising my granddaughter together. We had no one to turn to for help. Looming over my head during this time were thoughts of homelessness. Well-meaning people would tell me not to go the route of divorce because the courts were so biased against women. My lawyer was advising me that this was the way to ensure my status legally. Other people would inform me that the New York laws would have us divide everything equally and

I would be sure to lose my house. I learned to live one day at a time trusting God to help me. I thank the many friends who prayed for me at that time.

As our ministry of healing grew, the Lord saw to it that people were led to us who were able to assist us financially. One friend, Rose Benvenuto, in particular felt led by the Holy Spirit to pray specifically for my financial needs. She tells me all the time that God wants me to have the best and that God doesn't wish me to want for anything. She is always encouraging. When the House of Peace needed a car, she led the drive that enabled us to buy one. I know that God sent Rose to help me in my healing of want. Two Corinthians reads, "Indeed, everything is ordered for your benefit, so that the grace bestowed in abundance may bring greater glory to God because they who give thanks are many" (4:14). I am truly grateful to Rose, and God is glorified when someone like her reaches out and lifts someone else up with new hope for a better life. As she has given me confidence I am able to pass it on to hundreds of others. We are called to rally together and cheer on our friends who are dispirited because of financial deprivation. Thank you, Rose. I love you.

One day my friend and neighbor, Rinda Sternberg, who was aware of my fear of losing the house, suggested that I visualize the house with a ribbon around it and see it being presented to me as a gift from God. This became a daily exercise. As I envisioned my house with a great big red ribbon and bow around it, I thanked God in advance for the gift. I worked on letting go of being unforgiving, asking the Holy Spirit's help.

I centered myself through silent prayer and focused on the goodness of God in order to maintain my peace of mind. I prayed for both myself and my former spouse, asking only that God's perfect justice would prevail for both of us. I knew full well that God loved him just as much as He loved me.

My fears were a constant source of trouble to me. At these times I would turn to the power of affirmations. Affirmations were a great help in establishing faith in the goodness of God. The subconscious mind picks up what is being said and eventually negates the limiting voices that bring about fear. It deprograms the mind from negative thought patterns and instills good and healthy thought patterns. I would repeat affirmations over and over until the fears subsided, always asking the help of the Holy Spirit while doing so. Some of my favorite affirmations are: "Perfect love casts out all fear", "God works in mysterious ways, His wonders to perform." "The Lord is my Shepherd I shall not want." "God grants me abundance under grace in perfect ways."

I heard the phrase, "Fear is the darkroom where negatives are developed." Fear is our worst enemy and will block the flow of God's storehouse of gifts if we give it power. To also help me alleviate my fears I would fall asleep at night listening to affirmations on cassette tapes. Whenever I needed money, I would ask in the Name of Jesus, and, by golly, I would receive an unexpected gift from an unexpected source. I would also envision money falling from Heaven and sure enough the same thing would happen. I gave my daughter forty *dollars once during a time when my financial needs seemed to be great. She expressed concern because she knew how little I had for myself. I said to her flippantly so she wouldn't feel bad, "If I give this to you, I'll probably get it back one hundredfold." Much to my surprise, two days later I received a $400 check from an anonymous donor — it was the first and only $400 I ever received.*

The proceedings of my divorce took place over a number of years. In the meantime, our healing ministry was flourishing and growing by leaps and bounds; only those closest to me knew how I walked in faith. I believe now the reason my divorce took so long was because the Holy Spirit was working to ensure that the right judge would preside on the bench. As God's justice would have it, that is exactly what happened. I received my house as part of the divorce settlement. Praise God from whom all blessings flow! One of my favorite Scripture passages is "Look at the birds of the air: they neither sow nor reap. . . yet your Heavenly Father feeds them. Are not you of more value than they?"(Mt 6:26). There was a time when I thought I was less valuable, but my Heavenly Father has helped me to know that He is the Giver of all gifts. I need to keep my mind centered on Him and be vigilant over my attitudes. When limiting ideas start to tempt, I need to replace them with a vision of gifts, waiting to be received.

So, my dear readers, I leave you with the thought that God wants you to flourish. Let us pray that with God's help we can undo the blocks to the awareness of His abundance; that we will be shown how we can

Rise and Be Healed

improve our attitudes, especially the attitude of gratitude. There is more, there is so much more.
>   *I love you,*
>   *Maryanne Lacy*

Let Us Pray:

Heavenly Father, Jesus has told us, "Seek first His Kingship over you, His way of holiness, and all these things will be given you besides." Help us to realize the true meaning of prosperity based on this Scripture passage. We need your grace to develop our souls and express its talents so that we may discover our highest potential. Through the empowerment of the Holy Spirit, we ask to be in loving service to you and humankind. In doing so we will open ourselves to having all our needs met in bountiful measure. As we give so shall we receive. The more our needs are met by you so shall we bless and help others. Your gifts, Oh Lord, are an endless supply of bounty waiting to be received by us. Remove from our hearts and minds the blocks to receiving, for it seems You are more willing to give than we are to receive. I want to be open and receptive to enriching beliefs. My attitudes have not been helpful to me and I resist my own good by blaming you and others for my seeming want. I choose to let go of any tendency to blame anyone or anything.

I want to view all of Creation with a new outlook. I ask for a greater degree of faith and trust in your plan for my life. I desire and accept a new excitement and zeal for life. I look forward with eagerness to new insights and interests. Open my mind to an understanding of your abundant nature. I desire to let go of limiting ideas. I need the faith to look beyond the deception of impoverishment and contemplate your never-ending source of supply. I thank you, God, for the many friends who are sent by you to encourage me to believe in myself. I thank you for the wonderful gift of prayer in being able to come to you and know that you are present to me in my need. I praise you and thank you for your wonderful goodness to me. You have blessed me many times in my life and I have failed to recognize your loving hand guiding me. Your love has supported me time and time again. Thank you, Father, Son and Holy Spirit for blessing me so much. God is so Good!

> *"Who is like the Lord, Our God,*
> *From the dust he lifts up the lowly,*
> *From their misery he raises the poor to set them*
> *in the company of princes."*
> (Psalm 113)

Chapter 8

RISE AND BE HEALED OF GENERATIONAL BONDAGE

"Do not call anyone on earth your father. Only one is your father, the one in heaven" (Matthew 23:9).

During the years of our full-time involvement in praying with people for healing, we have made a number of breakthroughs during which we understood the healing process a little better. Our first breakthrough was an experience with Dr. Bernie Siegal when we discovered that there was more to cancer than just the physical symptoms. Another breakthrough came when we discovered how much co-dependence contributes to sickness and disease. Another one came when we met Dr. Ken McAll and discovered the impact of our family tree on illnesses which we may be experiencing in the present moment. Dr. Ken McAll wrote the book *Healing Our Family Tree* (Shelton Press, 1982), which has become the standard work on generational healing.

We have maintained throughout this book that many of the diseases and dysfunctions we experience in our lives are multi-generational. What this means is that our present problems only seem to arise from our immediate surroundings. When we investigate further, we find that many of these same problems have existed in our family history and they are being recycled in the present moment. We are not born into this world isolated from our family history. In some mysterious way, we carry that history around with us in our minds and bodies. We can experience the effects that our ancestry has had on us physically, psychologically, and spiritually.

It is obvious how much we have been affected biologically by our heredity. I inherited most of my physical characteristics from my father, but I manifest the personality of my mother. My father always had problems with his skin, but my mother had absolutely beautiful skin. Their six children were divided evenly between those with skin problems and those with beautiful skin. We know that we can inherit a disposition toward certain diseases such as heart problems, cancer, diabetes, etc. Often we see ourselves as victims of our inheritance because so much of our physical makeup has been handed down to us by our parents. We presume if a certain sickness is in our family history that there is nothing we can do to prevent it in our own lives. The good news of generational healing is that this presumption is not true. I know this from personal experience.

One of my earliest recollections was my father's fiftieth birthday. I was only about five years old at the time. Even in my child's mind I knew that there was something different about the party celebrating this event. When I asked what was the reason for the big celebration, I was told that my father had "made fifty," which meant that he had another twenty years to live. It seems that the family history of McCall men was that they either died of a heart attack before fifty, or they died in their seventies.

The McCall family tradition was evident in the fact that my father's father died of a heart attack at forty-eight; his brother died of a heart attack at forty-eight; and my brother died of a heart attack at forty-eight. So, what did I do when I reached forty-eight? I had a heart attack. Fortunately, by this time I knew a little about generational healing. As I lay in the intensive care unit, I realized that I had gone along with the "family flaw" and did what was expected of me, I immediately rejected my family tradition in the Name of Jesus Christ and affirmed that I choose life instead of death. I was acutely aware that I could choose whether to live or die. Although I had a serious heart attack, I went back to work in five months.

On an unconscious level, I was identifying with the "family flaw" and setting myself up to follow my ancestral heritage. It was not until I recognized what I doing, and made a conscious choice to renounce my family inheritance in the Name of Jesus Christ, that I was healed. Part of generational healing, is a prayer of deliverance in which we proclaim that we are not victims of our family history and that the power of Jesus Christ is greater than any family inheritance. Jesus told us, "Call no one on earth your Father; you have but one Father in heaven" (Mt 23:9). In telling us this, he was saying that all of us have a divine inheritance from our one Source of life. We can claim and appropriate that inheritance instead of the one we received from our earthly parent.

Generational healing is very similar to Jesus' parable about the Kingdom of Heaven being like a net which is thrown into the sea and collects fish of every kind (Mt 13:47-48). We are told that fishermen sit down and put into buckets what is good, and what is bad they throw away. This is also true with generational healing. We know that we come into this world as a "mixed bag." We are a combination of healthy and unhealthy characteristics. What we do is sit down with Jesus and keep what is good in our family history and throw away that which is destructive. We proclaim that we are not victims of our inheritance and that we have the power to pick and choose that which we want to keep and propagate in our family line and that which we want to stop.

Another form of generational healing has to do with our psychological inheritance. We know today that certain emotional pathologies have family roots. Depression can be a "gift" from an ancestor. Today we know so much more about how a dysfunctional family can be the root cause of the addictions, compulsions, and obsessions which plague and paralyze us individually and as a society. The more we study the dysfunctional family and examine the family trees of such families, the more we realize that the present generation is simply acting out the dysfunctions of previous generations.

When children have been "battered" by a parent, they are most likely to become "batterers" themselves when they become parents. In our ministry we hear all sorts of stories from people who swore that they would never treat their children the same way they were treated, but who find themselves behaving in exactly the same way their parents did toward their own children. This is a generational problem. Violent and abusive families seem to propagate themselves and until some members of those families make a decision to stop the insanity in their generation, it continues to be passed down to the next generation.

Another form of generational healing has to do with our cultural inheritance. Cultures are systems of practices and beliefs which are helpful in giving identity and structure to the lives of many people, but a culture can also cause many dysfunctions when accepted behaviors of the group encourage shame and addictions.

In her book, *For Your Own Good* (Farrar Straus, 1984), Alice Miller points out how the German family system, which was hierarchical and autocratic, made the acceptance of Adolf Hitler possible. At the Nuremberg trials, after World War II, hundreds of German soldiers and officers pleaded innocent to obvious crimes against humanity by saying that they were only doing what they were told to do. They could deny responsibility for what they did on the grounds that they were obedient to the system.

The disease of alcoholism can also be handed down culturally. Patterns of drinking have become lifestyles, not only for families, but also for nations. It is to the credit of Mikhail Gorbachev that he saw what alcoholism was doing to Russia and actually invited the spiritual program of Alcoholics Anonymous to come into his country to help with the crisis. In many cultures, excessive drinking is the way to express both happiness and sadness. The social acceptability of alcoholism is a generational problem which cries out for healing.

Much violence and prejudice in our society is generational. The hatred between certain groups of peoples goes back generations to causes which the present generation may not remember. It became part of the family inheritance and it has been accepted without challenging where it came from. So much of what we call national pride is simply national prejudice which has been handed down from one generation to the next. For example, Brother John Driscoll, C.F.C., Ph.D., President of Iona College, New Rochelle, NY, and an expert on Irish History, said that if England had decided to remain Catholic during the days of Henry VIII, Ireland would have gone Protestant. Generational disease can go very deep.

Now let us talk about the process of generational healing. Generational healing through prayer is based on the doctrine of the Communion of Saints. What this doctrine teaches is that all of us, living and deceased, are connected in some way. Saint Paul taught this doctrine under the name of the Mystical Body of Christ. This doctrine means that what we do here on earth has an effect on those who have gone over to the other side and vice versa. It means that we, today, can make "re-pair-ation" for the mistakes made in the past by our family members and change the effects these mistakes have made on the present generation.

Generational healing takes place in the context of the celebration of the Eucharist. Those participating in the Mass are asked to make out a family tree. We are all a product of four different family lines. It is good to know as much as possible about our family backgrounds. We encourage people to sit down with some of the elder family members while they are still alive and ask them specific questions about their family history. It is good to do this with a tape recorder and to put the entire conversation on tape. Explain to the elder members that it is extremely important that they reveal the "family secrets" because the present generation may be acting out conflicts buried in the past. Dysfunctions are propagated in the family line through denial. We can not afford to keep quiet about the behaviors and sicknesses, mental and physical, of past members in the family.

The importance of knowing our family tree cannot be over emphasized. Our happiness and peace on earth is not complete until our entire family is at peace. Saint Paul says that we are the Body of Christ, "if one part suffers, all the parts suffer with it; if one part is honored, all the parts share in the joy" (1 Cor 12:26). We should not treat our family history lightly and believe that things that happened long ago do not make any difference today. As a telephone company constantly reminds us, "We're all connected," and the things that happened in our family history may very well be repeating themselves today if we refuse to look at them and pray. The present generation may well be acting out the guilt, anger, and shame of the family line. Nothing can be healed that is not revealed.

Once we know as much as we can about our family history, there are four different movements that generational healing prayer takes. The first movement is thanksgiving. We need to express our thanks to our ancestors for all the good things we have received by way of heredity. Many of the family traits and characteristics we have received are good and beneficial to ourselves and others. It is appropriate to list and be mindful of those hereditary gifts. Some of these gifts may be physical such as: good health, a good immune system, athletic ability, etc. Some of them may include artistic abilities: singing, a love for nature, patriotism, spirituality, cooking skills. Any trait or characteristic which has obviously been passed down from one generation to the next for the benefit of many people is something to be thankful for. We should be grateful to our ancestors for the hard work they endured to give us a standard of living which we now enjoy. So the first movement of generational healing is to show appreciation for the good things we have received from our family line.

After we have paid our debt of gratitude to our ancestors, the second movement of healing is to take an inventory of those hereditary characteristics which are destructive and dysfunctional. Jesus told us to pray, "Deliver us from evil" (Mt 6:13). Generational healing now becomes a prayer of deliverance. We use the direction of the Holy Spirit and the authority of Jesus to cast out of the "collective consciousness" of our family anything that is presently harmful and destructive. These include all the addictions, obsessions, and compulsions which have been part of the family tradition such as: the physical, emotional, sexual, and religious abuses which have been acted out in the family. We cast out all the physical and psychological sicknesses which have manifested in the family line.

We pray with the boldness of Jesus, "Whatever went on before me in my family background that is destructive stops here! I reject it! I renounce it! I will have nothing to do with it! I will not pass it down to the next generation! I say this in the Name of Jesus Christ of Nazareth!" This prayer should not be said in a generalized way, but should be very specific. Name the exact characteristic which you want withdrawn from your family line and pray with boldness and confidence in the Name of Jesus Christ.

The prayer of deliverance is not a magical formula. It is an affirmation by which we break all ties with the past and the negative influence it has had on us. Like all prayer, it is said for ourselves first. For the prayer to be effective, we have to demonstrate in our own lives that these negative patterns of behavior no longer have power over us. Once we do this, our decision will have a positive influence on the rest of the family. AlAnon has an expression which expresses this well, "Your family's recovery begins with your own." As we demonstrate freedom from the past, our family reaps the benefit.

The third movement in generational healing is praying for our deceased relatives. Praying for the dead has been a religious tradition in both the East and the West. In the Judaic-Christian tradition prayer for the deceased has its roots in 2 Maccabees 12:43-46, where Judas Maccabee orders that expiatory sacrifices be offered for the slain soldiers "that they may be free from sin." This belief is also expressed in the Catholic teachings on Purgatory. The basic belief behind these teachings is that people can leave this world with "unfinished business," and that somehow we can make up for this deficiency by our prayers and forgiveness.

Saint Bonaventure, the great Franciscan Doctor of the Church, did not teach that Purgatory was a place of suffering, but, rather, it was a place of healing and completion. We can help "incomplete souls." Forgiveness is the best form of prayer we can offer to our ancestry. Many of our ancestors passed over to the other side with regret about things they should have done or said, but were left undone. We believe that we can free them from these disappointments by releasing all anger or bitterness that was left behind.

Generational healing is basically healing of relationships. We simply cannot afford to hold grievances against anyone living or deceased. Just because a person has died doesn't mean that our relationship with him/her has ended. It is never too late to be reconciled. Jesus told us, "Whatever you bind on earth will be bound in heaven; whatever you loose on earth will be loosed in heaven" (Mt 18:18). We free both ourselves and our deceased relatives when we forgive them and give them to God.

There are certain deceased relatives that demand special attention. These are relatives who died suddenly or by violence. It is often apparent that they left this world in a state of conflict. We are concerned with relatives who committed suicide. Fortunately, in our day, we know a lot more about the mental and emotional state that a person must be in to commit suicide than has been known before. It wasn't that long ago when the Catholic Church believed that if a person committed suicide that he/she sinned seriously and was deprived of a Christian funeral and was buried in a separate plot in the cemetery. Now we know that such a person must be filled with many feelings of self-condemnation, despair, and helplessness to commit such an act of self-centered violence to himself or herself.

The deception of suicide is that death is going to be a release of the problems and anxieties that presently plague us. The tragedy of this belief is that the person simply carries these problems over to the other side. Whatever we are experiencing here, we will experience there. Suicide does not solve any problems, it is merely a change in geography. This means that we, the living relatives here, still have an obligation to help that person. We can do this through forgiveness and understanding. We can release the person who committed suicide to Jesus and trust that whatever unfinished business this person had on earth can be worked out with Jesus on the other side. We are not to imagine this person suffering in hell for all eternity. The person was suffering a hell when he/she thought that suicide would end the anguish. Now we can help by our forgiveness and the support of our prayers.

It is my personal belief that souls of the deceased are not far away from us. They are on another plane of existence, but they are not separated from us in an irrevocable way. I have heard too many stories from people who have experienced the presence of a deceased loved one to believe that have gone far away from us. In a healing prayer ministry, people reveal to us things they ordinarily would not. I have been told stories of seeing and hearing deceased relatives usually right after they died. I believe every one of these stories. I have no doubt that the people on the other side want us to help them and they want to help us. I do not believe in death. I believe that someone moves from one form of existence to another, but there is no end to life. In one of the Prefaces of the Mass of the Resurrection it says, "Life is changed, not ended." I believe this. I also believe that the close relationship we have with the deceased relatives makes generational healing possible.

Another area of generational healing is abortions, miscarriages, and stillborn babies within the family. These children are part of the family tree and must be treated as persons who need healing. It is beyond the scope of this book to explain how this can happen. We highly recommend another book, however, called *Healing the Greatest Hurt*, by Dennis and Matthew Linn and Sheila Fabricant (Paulist Press, 1985). Those of us in the healing prayer ministry are constantly asked to pray with women who have had an abortion and, maybe ten or twenty years later, are just beginning to face the guilt and shame that arises from such an act of violence. Denial runs high on this issue and it is so important in healing the family tree to bring these babies to Jesus.

In his healing practice, Doctor Kenneth McAll has discovered the power of the Eucharist to bring about generational healing. It has been a long tradition in the Catholic Church to have Masses celebrated for the deceased, but it became such a routine gesture that the full significance of the Eucharist as prayer has been lost. When generational healing is prayed for in the context of the Eucharist, the family setting of a meal is emphasized. The Eucharist is a meal set on a table, the altar, around which the family gathers. Just as we celebrate Thanksgiving, Christmas, and other family events by eating and drinking around a table, so the prayer of the Eucharist is celebrated. It is a powerful sign of healing. Just as around the dining room table much of the family's dysfunctions were manifested, so now, around the altar with Jesus as Host, these dysfunctions can be healed.

This brings us to the final movement of generational healing, praying for the living. As we look at our dysfunctional families, we wonder if there is any possibility of healing. So many living family members manifest the "family flaw." However, our experience has been that generational healing works. In our ministry, we celebrate a healing Mass on the First Saturday of every month. On the First Saturday of November, as close as possible to the Feast of All Saints (November 1st) and All Souls (November 2nd) we celebrate a Generational Healing Mass. We have everyone fill out a "family tree" and we celebrate a Mass of Resurrection found in the Appendix of Dr. Kenneth McAll's book, *Healing the Family Tree* (Shelton Press 1982). During the Prayer of the Faithful, we follow the four movements of generational healing: thanksgiving, prayer of deliverance, prayer for the deceased, and prayer for the living. We have received wonderful witness letters about the power of this Eucharist. Families have reported almost instantaneous changes, while others have noticed a gradual change for the good within their families.

It is amazing what happens as we come to terms with our family history, as we reveal our family secrets, as we reconcile ourselves with our deceased relatives, and as we bring our family flaws to Jesus. The bondage of the past begins to loosen and the beliefs in victimization begin to weaken. We see ourselves more as children of God than just children of two earthly parents. We, the living, are more at home with our family of origin as we feel the freedom from the oppression of our family's past history. I do not know exactly how it works, I only know that I have seen that it does.

Father Peter McCall

Reflections and Sharing

RISE AND BE HEALED OF GENERATIONAL BONDAGE

My little granddaughter, Jessica, has lived with me since she was an infant. I noticed that at a very early age she was quite fearful of some people and yet very trusting of others. She was less than a year old when she was fearful of large round objects such as balloons and basketballs. When she was about two she was frightened of a toy dog that did tricks. This problem of fear, as Father Peter has pointed out, is a multi-generational enigma. Who knows where or when it begins. The book, The Secret Life of the Unborn Child *by Thomas Verney, MD, with John Kelly (Dell Publishing, 1981), reports on the research which has been done with a number of expectant parents. The book is based on two decades of medical research on the unborn child. This research reveals some startling facts, especially that an unborn baby is an active, feeling human being, extremely sensitive to the parents' feelings about him or her. I firmly believe that the fears of many generations past can be passed on and on and propagated until someone in a particular generation decides to do something about getting healed. I think this is also true of violence and all dysfunctions.*

183

As I have already mentioned in previous chapters, I come from generations of violent ancestry. Anger was the predominant emotion shown in my family. We were raised on fear and guilt by fearful and angry adults who had fearful and angry parents, and so on. About fifteen years ago, I was going through great anguish regarding the issue of generational violence. Not only had I been raised in an angry atmosphere but had even created one through marriage and it was too much for me to bear. I cried out to God in my confusion and pain, "When is this violence ever going to end?" How I yearned for peace of mind. In my distress I was anything but peaceful, but suddenly I felt a miraculous calm come over me. I felt as though someone had stopped me dead in my tracks and in the mystical quiet I was urged to listen. The thought and words were spoken to me that I had been chosen to be the one to break through the generational barriers of violence in my family line. I was being asked to learn the ways of peace; that peace begins with me. "Blessed are the peacemakers, for they shall be called children of God" (Mt 5:9).

Since then I have seen, in hindsight, the fruits of that calling. It has not always been easy, but I know that I have made a difference. For instance, one time an incident caused a difficulty with three of my children and myself. If I had not taken time to walk away from that volatile encounter and sit in quiet there would have been a recycling of anger and bitterness. I sat in my quiet room and asked for the peace that passes all understanding to come upon me. I spoke to the Holy

Spirit and said, "And now I ask that the peace that is indwelling in each of my children be stirred up and I join with them in the realm of the Holy Spirit for peace in this situation." When I walked out of my room I knew what I knew. Sure enough there were apologies all around and regrets for quick tempers. We were able to sit down at the supper table in peace and harmony. It was over. Praise God! To be the intercessor for stopping the madness from continuing in the ancestry requires a personal, individual commitment to prayer — to know God and to work with Him in cooperating with His plan for peace in the world. He needs us, dear Readers. We can make a difference.

I think that as intercessors for our family line we are also asked to make reparation. I don't mean this in the sense of self-punishment, but rather in repair-action. Father Peter mentions this form of healing in terms of the mistakes of our ancestry. For example, there is a great deal of alcoholism in our family tree and in the children's family ancestry. Thank God I was spared and do not have an addiction to alcohol. My addictions are more in the co-dependency area. However, about five years ago I was inspired to give up any form of alcohol for the rest of my life as a form of prayer and fasting for the healing of alcohol addiction in the family. With the grace of God I have been true to that and because of the personal nature of the subject can only say I have seen the fruits of it.

Father Peter has pointed out that family diseases, in his case heart disease, can be renounced as part of the generational healing process. In my case, when I was going through the healing of breast cancer, I was not fully conscious of the fact that cancer was in the family line. My paternal grandmother was supposed to have died of breast cancer at a very young age. It was something that was not talked about much. Family secrets can also be generational. However, I do pray that cancer will not be passed on to future generations and whenever we have a Generational Healing Mass said for the family, I always include cancer.

Recently, a close friend was diagnosed as having Parkinson's disease, a chronic, progressive disorder of the central nervous system. He was devastated to say the least. In addition to the concern for himself was the anxiety that it might be passed on to his children and his grandchildren, since Parkinson's can be inherited. In praying with our friend, we discovered that his grandfather had all the symptoms, but no one diagnosed it in those days and it was just accepted as something his grandfather had. Another connection was the fact that one of his children had a bout of multiple sclerosis approximately thirteen years earlier. Multiple sclerosis is a disease of the nervous system, mainly the brain and spinal cord. This disease can also be inherited. Thank God, his child has been healed as a result of healing prayer. She has been in remission for over ten years. Ironically, his wife's family had amyotrophic lateral sclerosis, otherwise known as Lou Gehrig's disease. The muscle degeneration in this disease is initiated when certain nerve cells, known as motor neurons, begin to die. So we see that in this family line, a particular disease was already passed down three generations in various forms. We brought the family together for a Generational Healing Mass, praying for the healing of past ancestry, the present generation, and future generations. We continue to pray with our friend for his healing. After the Generational Healing Mass he experienced a great release from the burden that this disease might be passed on. At his last medical report, the doctors were amazed that most of his symptoms were gone.

The current data on Alzheimer's disease is that it is recognized as having several forms: one, for example, strikes before the age of 55 and runs in families. Researchers are already certain that genes are at work. We have a number of people who come to our healing services who are concerned, and rightly so. Since there is currently no known cure, we can have the comfort of coming before the only One who has a cure and can redeem the genetic tendency to disease. Someone in the family line is called to be aware and to act on behalf of the rest of the family in praying for the healing of all inherited disorders.

The third movement of generational healing that Father Peter touches on is praying for our deceased relatives. He tells us of "incomplete souls." About twelve years ago, I was sitting in a lounge chair in my yard relaxing. It was summertime and a clear sunny day. I became aware of an electricity (buzzing) around me and I sensed I was being summoned to have a conversation with God. I left my lounging chair and went into my quiet room. Nothing like this had ever happened to me before, but nonetheless, I inquired, "What is it, Jesus?"

I was quite startled when I distinctly heard the voice of my step-uncle, who is dead. I was particularly fond of this uncle even though he was not a blood relative. He said to me, "Maryanne, I need your prayers." Whether he had anything more to say I don't know because I was so astonished, I must have cut off the connection. After much thought I prayed for him and I also asked his sister, my stepmother, to have Masses said for him. When I expressed concern as to why I heard this, she simply replied that I was the one who was listening. Can it be our friends and relatives are trying to get through to us and directing us to pray for them? If what Father Peter says is true, that there is really no separation on a spiritual plane, then this would make sense. After all, in this world, if a friend is hurting at some particular time, all they have to do is pick up the telephone and ask us to pray for them. So our friends on the other side have to use the form of connection that is available to them. Some of us have to be listening.

When Father Peter and I began to realize the powerful importance of generational healing, we decided to include a Generational Healing Mass in every workshop and retreat. We also decided to have a public one each year, near the feast of All Saints and All Souls Day in November. We had our first Mass about five years ago on the first Saturday of November at Blessed Sacrament Chapel. I fasted and prayed for about a week prior to the Mass. On the morning of the Mass, I experienced a vibration going through my entire body. I do not know how to explain it, but I was not here in this realm. I saw in a vision, or maybe it was real, I don't know, a large crowd of people. They were veiled, that is, not clear, and they were all shapes and sizes and ages. I experienced a deep sadness and a trembling. I realized through some form of understanding that these people were relatives of those who would be present at the Mass that afternoon. The message being relayed to me was that this multitude wanted to express regret for harm done to those still living. They were expressing sorrow and wanted, and very much needed, forgiveness. There seemed to be a great deal of unfinished business and some wanted to tell their loved ones they loved them even though they had never expressed it in this life. This was an amazing discovery to me. To be sure, I shared it at the right time during the Generational Healing Mass. There were many tears that day and a release of unforgiveness. I believe many souls were released and put at rest because of those prayers, especially the prayers throughout the Mass.

I have been involved in many personal generational healings and have had Masses said for my own family. I mentioned earlier that my mother died at an early age. After a particular Healing Mass — not generational — I noticed a woman waiting for me to finish praying. I knew this woman only slightly at the time. I had seen her at the healing services. When I finished, she approached me cautiously and didn't seem too sure as to what to say. She proceeded to inform me that while I was praying for the congregation from the altar, she began to rest under the power of the Holy Spirit and she became quite puzzled because a woman's voice interrupted her and identified herself as my *mother. She wanted to ask my forgiveness for leaving me when I was so young. She wanted me to know that she was praying for me. I looked at this woman in astonishment and said, "Did you know that my mother died when I was two?" The woman was just as astonished and said, "No, Maryanne, I know nothing about your personal life." We marveled together and I thanked her for telling me. This news brought me so much comfort and happiness that for weeks I rejoiced.*

About two weeks after this event, I was praying during our weekly Tuesday noon healing service when one of our prayer team members, Frances DiFede, approached me and told me she had seen a young woman with brown hair, holding a baby in her arms on my left side, and she was interceding for me. She also saw the presence of the Blessed Mother on my right side. Frances did not know about the message from my mother two weeks previous; I had not shared it with anyone but Father Peter. Again, this brought me great joy and consolation. Frances did not know that my mother had died in childbirth and that the baby died as well. The baby was in my mother's arms. The power of Generational Healing Masses is not limited to time and space.

Interestingly, I received tickets for my birthday this year to a Broadway performance of "The Secret Garden." The story is of a haunted man named Archibald, who is still grieving for his dead wife after ten years. She was quite beautiful and the joy of his life. Just before she was about to give birth to their first child, she fell from a branch of a tree in her special garden and delivered prematurely. She died in childbirth but the child lived, although it was quite sickly and always close to death. Archibald rejected the child. He even hired someone to take care of it. His wife had also left behind a sister whom she hadn't seen since she married Archibald. There was a rift between them before she died, so there was unfinished business. Then the sister died in the play and her child, Mary Lennox, was sent to live with Archibald as the closest living relative. In the background one can see how the spirits of two dead sisters are guiding and directing Mary to find the little boy and help bring about reconciliation between father and son. There is a particularly touching scene that struck home with me. In a dream, Archie is granted a reunion with his dead wife, the beautiful Lily, and she is able to tell him how sorry she is for having left him, that she didn't know how much it would have hurt him. She asks pardon and forgiveness and requests of him that he take care of their son because the child needs his love. You can be sure there were tears shed in the audience, including mine. It sounded all too familiar. I was very much aware that the little girl, Mary Lennox, was the repairer of relationships in her family of both the living and the dead.

Recently, we gave a retreat in Monte Alvernon Retreat House, Appleton, Wisconsin. At the end of the retreat we invited the retreatants to share. A young woman, Linda Sieber, shared with us a powerful event that took place in her family as a direct result of a Generational Healing Mass. At a previous retreat, she filled out a family tree and placed it on the altar during the Mass. She especially prayed for her mother and father. Her father had abandoned the family when Linda was about seven years old. She didn't know him very well because he wasn't around much before he left. However, through the years, she mourned the loss of her father and wondered about him. He had been missing for over thirty years. No one seemed to know where he had gone and Linda and her brother and sisters always hoped to hear some word of him. Right after this Generational Healing Mass, Linda's mother had to go to the social security office to inquire about benefits. Through the office's computer her former husband's name appeared. It showed where he had lived, that he had remarried and that he had died several years earlier. Through this information, Linda's brother wrote to the town requesting a death certificate which carried the name of the cemetery where the father was buried, in Minnesota.

By sheer coincidence Linda and her husband, were planning to go to Minnesota to pick up their daughter, who was there on tour. While at the grave, Linda felt awkward, remembering she did not know her father very well. But, because of her faith in Jesus and her own convictions, she felt it was only natural to forgive him for abandoning her and the family. In fact, she felt she had to intercede for him and pray for his well-being and salvation. Linda recalls having a strong desire to know he was with Jesus. She presented him to God explaining that he too had been an abandoned child. He, in fact, had been abandoned by his own mother at the age of four and Linda knew that his life had been very difficult. Her compassion for her father was indeed a mir-

acle of salvation. Instinctively, Linda knew that it was not right to hold any unforgiveness toward him. She prayed, "God you are not limited by time and space and somehow a daughter praying for a father who abandoned her must count for something." After that she felt a closure on her relationship with her father and she experienced a sense of freedom and peace. For many years, Linda had longed for information about her father and she had mourned the loss of his presence and love. It was now finished and complete; the healing had come. Praise God from whom all blessings flow.

I love you,
Maryanne Lacy

Let Us Pray:

Father, there is so much mystery concerning this subject of Generational Healing. We do know, however, that Jesus Christ, our living Savior, has poured out his life for us so that we might live. Because of the Resurrection, we can be assured that we do not die. We just put aside this familiar form and enter another dimension of existence. We are but a thought away; still living but unseen. We are comforted by this knowledge and we seek to be reconciled through the act of forgiveness to those loved ones in our family who have gone beyond, but left without finishing their mission. We need to grieve and mourn our losses and we so desire to let go and get on with the subject of living.

Father, Jesus has admonished us in Holy Scripture to call no one on earth our Father. We have only one Father, that is you, our Unconditionally loving parent. You who created us in love to be a member of the Kingdom of Peace. Since you are our true Parent, we acknowledge that we cannot inherit any evil from you. We cannot inherit sickness, poverty, depression, or addictions from you. We cannot even inherit death from you, because you are a God of the living. We proclaim liberation from the world's limitations through our inheritance as children of the Most High God. We thank you for the opportunities you have given us to become peacemakers for ourselves, our loved ones both living and dead and for future generations. Because Jesus has given us the power to forgive, we let go and unleash anyone and everyone, and we pray for those deceased that they may also be emancipated from the bondage of regret and remorse. May they be granted the grace of forgiving themselves and also be aware that we, in turn, forgive them their offenses against us. We give them permission to be free as we, in turn, are freed.

Through the Redemption of Our Lord and Savior we can return to our original state of union with God. All Glory and Honor to God, the Father, Jesus Christ, our Redeemer and our Magnificent Advocate, the Holy Spirit. We have the victory, in the name of the Father, Son and Holy Spirit. Amen.

On the Road to Wholeness

January 23, 1991
Father Peter and Maryanne:

A million thanks. Over the past three years you and Maryanne have taken me on a wonderful journey to know the Lord, the true knowing of His infinite, unconditional love for us. There is no greater feeling or human emotion than pleasing the Lord and feeling the Holy Spirit upon us. The journey was and will continue to be incredible. Yes, there was a lot of pain, the pain of releasing, letting go, detoxifying from the past, healing the child within and allowing that child to grow with me. It's like detoxifying from food, drugs, or alcohol. The process is Hell as we are getting rid of the garbage and the junk. As the body would detoxify and feel this pain, so does the mind and the heart as we detoxify from the hurts, the abandonment, the fears, the put-downs and all the negative feelings and actions of a dysfunctional family.

I never knew how much negativity I had lived with for almost 40 years. You and Maryanne literally saved my life. If it were not for the two of you, no, the three of you — you, Maryanne and the Lord, I would never have made it. In addition to all the wonderful friends that fill the House of Peace with the Hearts of Love. These last four and one-half years plus of being a caregiver for mom after her massive stroke and then going through it again six months and six days later when my Father suffered his massive stroke would have been overwhelming for me without the two of you and everyone's prayers. There is so much that has transpired, changed and been lifted from me, including healing the troubled mother-daughter relationship.

Last June 1990, at the first Saturday Healing Mass Maryanne laid her hands on my chest and prayed over me. After Maryanne left I could still feel hands on my chest. It left me wondering, and then I knew; I could feel the hands of the Holy Mother, I felt and saw the folds of her gown and the words shall forever remain in my soul and be pressed upon my heart: "These hands, this love are giving you all the love that was withheld, not shown to you, through your life, and as you take care of your mother, you, in turn, are giving her and showing her the love that had been withheld from her through her childhood. I am using you." I can not begin to describe the peace, joy and gentleness of that moment.

Father Peter, it has happened again. Yesterday afternoon when I came up for anointing, you very gently put your left hand on my cheek. There are no words to describe the total peace I felt. As I was driving home I could still feel that peace and unconditional love. As I meditated on it later, these were the words that were gently laid on my soul and inscribed on my heart: "In that touch, Lorraine, was all the love and acceptance that was withheld from you for most of your life. That was my hand." I knew that had been the hand of God you placed upon me, as gentle as angels' wings. The words continued, "I love you, my child, and your life begins anew from this day forward. Do you finally believe? Know that I AM with you, have always been with you and will always be with you. You are born again this day."

I was at peace and all the garbage and junk of the past 40 years had been drained away and replaced with total, unconditional love. In that moment of His time, there was no past, just a bright, rosy, abundant now and future." . . . where do I begin to tell a story of how sweet a love can be. . ." Can it be almost two years since April of 1989 when Maryanne was led to send Diane Harkin, a wonderful angel of love and light into my life — a gift — to my side to minister to me as I was going through "a total breakdown of my heart" right there in my seat? It was that Saturday that Maryanne received the word of knowledge that there was some-one here whose heart was broken, just totally broken in two. Diane gently led me up and I completely broke down in front of you, God and everyone. Well that began an incredible tense journey of detoxifying and healing. It began a wonderful friend-ship with an angel right here on earth — Diane.

From the bottom of my heart to the tip of my soul, I thank you all for your love, your help, your guidance and your pray-ers. You truly are gifts to me from God. God bless each and everyone of you for-ever and ever and ever. You are truly shining lights of His love.

All my love,
Lorraine Taliani
Mt. Kisco, NY

Chapter 9

WITNESS LETTERS

Thank you, Jesus

November 1990
Dear Father Peter and Maryanne,

I am writing this letter to openly witness how I was touched by the healing power of our Lord and Savior, Jesus Christ.

In May, 1979, I underwent surgery at Albert Einstein Hospital at which time a biopsy was taken from a large growth in the lymph gland under my right arm. The diagnosis revealed the growth to be a malignant tumor in the lymph gland. The tumor under my arm was approximately the size of an orange and was not getting smaller.

Meanwhile, my wife had heard about the Charismatic Renewal and we attended our first prayer meeting at our parish, Annunciation Church, in Yonkers, NY. For the next five Thursdays we attended the prayer meetings. I told the members about my condition and at the end of the meetings they would gather around me, lay their hands on me, and pray for my healing. This always gave me a great feeling of renewal, love, and hope. It was at one of these meetings that I was told of Father Peter McCall's Healing Mass.

It was Father Peter's first Healing Mass held at Mercy College on the Feast of the Sacred Heart of Jesus, in June 1979. It was the first time Fr. Peter McCall and Maryanne Lacy prayed with me. My mother-in-law and my wife were with me and we felt very optimistic that something good would happen.

Father Peter and Maryanne came to my home on several occasions during June 1979 to pray for my healing. They would pray in tongues and soak me in prayer. Maryanne would hold her hand on my tumor and Father Peter would have his hands on my back and they would pray and sing. During a prayer session at my home, we witnessed a physical manifestation of the Spirit's healing power. Maryanne's hands started to vibrate and I could feel the warmth in her hand as she held it against my tumor. This occurred on several visits thereafter. Towards the end of June, my tumor was found to have shrunk somewhat in size. This occurred without any medical treatment — just healing prayer.

After many weeks of testing, the doctors were unable to find any sign of a primary cancer cell. But they decided to perform radiation treatment on the tumor. The tumor responded very quickly to the radiation and continued to shrink in size. I knew the healing power had already been working inside of me and that it was the healing power of Jesus Christ.

I fully recovered from my condition. My sickness enabled me to learn about Jesus Christ in a way I would have never known him. He is not a distant God, but someone you can talk to. He hears and answers your prayers. I always think about how I was healed and I thank God every day for my healing. Thank you, Father Peter and Maryanne for your prayers!

Frank Civitano
Yonkers, NY

Praise the Sacred Heart of Jesus

February 25, 1991
Dear Father Peter and Maryanne,

I want to thank you both for all you have done for me and my family. You have helped open my heart to the healing power of Jesus and enlightened me to a special devotion I now have to the Sacred Heart of Jesus

I always thought of myself as religious because I tried to go to Mass daily. I prayed to God in a somewhat distant way. Then my husband, Frank, developed a malignant tumor and I experienced Jesus in a way I never did before. Jesus' presence in Frank's healing was no longer distant, but near. He experienced physical manifestations of soaking prayer. Your many visits to our home and healing prayers after Mass helped us experience Jesus' healing power.

One morning I was praying by a statue of the Sacred Heart in my Church and heard the words "Go home, your husband is healed, and you will be too. . ." I knew then Frank was healed, but I wondered what I was to be healed from. A few months later, I found out I was pregnant, but I was having a lot of problems with the pregnancy. Frank was having radiation and his doctor asked me what my thoughts were about abortion. I told him I wouldn't think of it. I knew God would take care of me. I could have lost the baby at any time since the baby was in a transverse position and I had placenta previa. They thought I would need an emergency Caesarian, but I delivered a healthy, normal, beautiful baby boy at full term without a Caesarian. You were constantly praying for me and soaking me in prayer at healing services and prayer meetings. I will never forget those times.

My son, Angelo, will be eleven on March 16th. He is a tall, handsome boy. Five years after Angelo's birth, I had a daughter, Francine, who is five years old now. God bless you both in your ministry! We all love you.

Love, Rosemarie Civitano

Baby's Healing

February, 1991
Dear Father Peter and Maryanne,

We are writing this letter to thank you and the House of Peace for all of your prayers and your kindness.

When our daughter was first born we discovered that she had an imperferated anus. We discussed surgery with the doctor and decided to wait until she was at least six months old before doing anything in hopes of it moving back into place on its own.

When Carolyn was two weeks old, the doctor found she had a heart murmur and sent us to a specialist. We prayed that it was just a simple murmur like many children are born with. The specialist told us Carolyn had a pulmonary stenosis, a narrowing of the valve in the heart. He said it wasn't bad but needed to be watched.

We were relieved, but still concerned, so we did a lot of praying. we thanked God for giving us Carolyn and asked Him for her good health. We took Carolyn for a sonogram of her heart every other month. Each time we went the valve was found to be closing more and more. By the time Carolyn was six months old, the narrowing was worse and they wanted to perform balloon surgery to open the valve. We took her for another opinion; the conclusion was the same, surgery was needed.

About a month before Carolyn was to have surgery, Greg was working at Maryanne's home. He talked to her about Carolyn's condition and came home with the book, An Invitation to Healing. We read through the book and decided to go to one of the Healing Masses at Blessed Sacrament in Yonkers.

We went to the Mass two weeks before the surgery date. The Mass was beautiful. Father Peter called us up to the altar and we all prayed over Carolyn, touching her heart and her rectum. Then we sat down with one of the ladies that was on the altar and said a prayer together. The woman asked us if we were going to have her tested again before surgery; she had felt something happening that day. Being there gave us a wonderful warm feeling.

Well, two weeks later we went to Boston for Carolyn's heart surgery. The date of the surgery was to be September 29, 1989 and pretesting was scheduled for the 28th. The morning of the 28th came, and before going to the hospital, Greg looked at Carolyn and said not to worry, because we would be going home tonight.

We went to the hospital and they did all kinds of pretesting. The last test was a sonogram of the heart. They put Carolyn to sleep and took the sonogram. The doctor informed us that Carolyn's condition had reversed itself and she wouldn't need the surgery after all. We were so happy we thanked the doctor and he said not to thank him but to thank someone else. We thanked God that day and every day since.

We went back home and took Carolyn to the doctor to check on the status of her imperferated anus. By that time it had somehow moved back on its own. We took her for two other opinions. The conclusion was that she did not need surgery at that time. Two of the doctors said they felt she can live a normal life just the way she was.

Our family and the people from the House of Peace helped Gregory and I to always believe in God's healing power and has helped us in healing our daughter.

Carolyn is now almost two years old and is doing wonderfully. We would like to thank everyone at the House of Peace and our family and friends for all the love and prayers extended to us. We pray for all of you and hope that our story will encourage and help others to believe in the wonderful love and healing power of God our Father. Thank you.

Sincerely,
Sharon and Greg Shuluk

Healing Through Intercession

July 6, 1990
Dear Maryanne:

My first encounter with the House of Peace healing ministry was several weeks ago when I was introduced to a healing service at Blessed Sacrament on a Tuesday at noon by a dear friend, Rosejean Castriota. Rosejean knew of my concern for my son, Stephen, who from infancy suffered from asthma, allergies and eczema. This concern only deepened when not too long before my attending my first healing service, Stephen was operated on for cataracts on one of his eyes. My anxiety for him be came more intense since I was not only concerned about the slow pace of his healing, but also about his mental state. He has had many disappointments in his relatively short life of twenty years because of the conditions described. Stephen is not a communicative type of person and became even less so when we discovered he had to have surgery on both eyes. I could not longer control my sorrow for him and often cried after the doctor informed us; I would cry especially during the Consecration of the Mass. I thought to myself how horrendous the pain must have been for our Blessed Mother when she heard and saw the lies, physical abuse and crucifixion of her Son. She was my only consolation, and still the tears often come.

The day I came to the healing service and you were speaking in tongues, you asked if there was someone in the audience who had asthma or a lung problem. I, the only one, responded by telling you that I was here for my son, who had asthma. During the anointing with the oil, I said little to you, or barely blurted out his illnesses and the recent surgery to you because I became so emotional, I could not control my tears. Your touch with the holy oil led to my resting in the Holy Spirit. I came away from the service that day a different person and this has not changed. I came away more confident knowing that my son's eye would heal properly. That very afternoon at 3:30 P.M., we had an appointment with another eye surgeon for a second opinion as to why the eye was so slow in healing. The doctor told us the surgery was fine and that the slow healing process was typical of youngsters who have asthma and allergies. I know that God intervened here to avoid my son experiencing another disappointment in life. He has since totally healed and has almost perfect vision without glasses.

My son is scheduled for the second operation on July 26, hence one of the reasons I am writing to you. If you could find a moment on that day, would you and Father Peter take a moment to pray along with our family and friends for its success also. I realize you must have busy schedule and this type of surgery technologically has come a long way, and there are people with greater illnesses and greater suffering, but he is my son and I feel deeply for him; love him and want the best for him, which are all the prayers we can get especially from people such as yourself and Father Peter whom God has given a special gift. Even as I write this, the tears flow.

Finally, the second reason for writing is to thank you for the fruits of your gift. I can find no other way to express how I feel. God Bless your ministry. I hope to see more of you and Father Peter once August allows you to resume your schedule here, in Yonkers.

Sincerely yours,
Carmine Forlenza
Yonkers, NY

Healing Through Perserverance

Dear Fr. Peter and Maryanne:

I just want to tell you what a wonderful experience it was for me to be embraced by your ministry. When I first became ill, around January 1989, my husband, Bob, and I went to many doctors. No one seemed to know what was wrong with me. My health kept failing and my left lung had collapsed. I went for all kinds of chest, lung, bone and abdomen scans, and nothing could be diagnosed. It was then that a wonderful man, named Tony Difley, introduced me to the House of Peace.

I felt I was always close to the Lord, but when I came to your services I could feel the strength and warmth of His love surrounding me. Maryanne, you and Fr. Peter prayed over me during the next few months. I was in and out of the hospital for many tests and biopsies during that time. Then, in March, I went for a lung biopsy and spent five days in the hospital.

I was released on Saturday, the first Saturday in the month of April. As we left the hospital I was very upset. My surgeon had found an inoperable large mass that was forcing my left lung to stay collapsed, but they still could not diagnose my condition or treat me. Bob and I decided we would go to Mass and the healing service before we went home. That Saturday, Fr. Peter prayed over me with Diane Harkin and the Lord spoke to me through them. I went home with such a feeling of trust and belief. I knew God was good and He would take care of me. If He could reach out to me in such a low time in my life, by bringing me into your loving community, I knew somehow He would carry me through whatever I was facing. You and Fr. Peter continued to pray with me and everyone around me held me in their prayers.

Finally, it was the end of May, my lung was still collapsed and my condition was rapidly deteriorating. My doctor called, he had finally heard some news. I was to go for another biopsy. This time they were removing a lymph node. I had the surgery performed and three days later found out I had Hodgkins Lymphoma. The doctors were very optimistic, and as my surgeon said, "Maryann, you are very lucky, you have the best cancer, God must have heard everyone's prayers." I started treatments in June. Both you and Fr. Peter continued to pray over me at every healing service. I believe through you both, God stretched His hand out and held me for the next eleven months. He showered me with the love and prayers of so many wonderful people and carried me forward over every obstacle until I heard that wonderful word 'normal'. All my tests turned out normal. What a great celebration we had, with the Lord in our hearts.

Thank you, Fr. Peter, Maryanne, and the House of Peace congregation. I'm sure God holds you all in a very special place in His heart and so do I.

Love you,
Maryann and Bob Trabucco
Seaford, NY

Jesus at My Side

July 15, 1988
Dear Father McCall and Maryanne,

I first became aware of the House of Peace when I was waiting to be operated on for endometrial cancer (uterine cancer) at Columbia Presbyterian Hospital.

I had requested to attend Mass and it would be an understatement to say I was

213

an emotional wreck. They sent this very nice man to take me to Mass. (He volunteers his services every Sunday). When we were returning from the service, he asked if there was anything he could do to help. I explained to him that the doctor found I had cancer of the lining of the uterus. He said to me, "Let us pray." He put his arms around me and as I cried, he prayed. In my life, I have never heard anyone pray with such meaning, emotion and love. He told me he would send his wife to see me. He said she was a good God-loving woman and very active in the House of Peace healing group. She was a nurse at this very hospital, and she, too, had cancer of the cervix ten years ago and she is fine now. I felt that he was a gift from God. His wife came, as he promised, the following day. She prayed over me and gave me nutritional advice. She assured me that our Lord, Jesus, loved me. I was not alone, Jesus would be at my side through my ordeal. She was right. I believed the Lord sent these two wonderful people to help me go through the worst time in my life. I thank Bridie and Pat Monaghan with all my heart. I was alone, frightened — they took my hand and showed me the way.

They told me about the Healing Mass services at Blessed Sacrament Chapel, and as soon as I was able, I started to attend.

I had good doctors, but deep in my heart I knew my faith was in the Lord. He was the one who was going to cure me. I always prayed for our Lord, Jesus' divine blessing for myself and friends who were in need of his help. But, I always felt that there were people who were in need much more than I, and, as Father Peter McCall always tells us, I felt unworthy.

On that special Saturday, as Maryanne was praying, I, too, prayed, "Please Lord, please cure me. . . My Lord, my Jesus, please cure me." I kept repeating it. I couldn't believe my ears as Maryanne started to describe this woman who was being cured of cancer at that moment. It can't be me! It can't be me! I was in shock. My daughter, who was seated next to me was nudging me. It was me! I was overwhelmed. I finally stood up. I don't know how I made it to the altar, I couldn't see through the tears. I went to see my doctors and they said that everything looked fine. The world may not acknowledge the healing that I have received. Doctors, as professionals, are cautious in stating that "everything is fine." However, within my heart, I know that I was healed by our Lord Jesus, my savior.

Blessed is our Lord Jesus and his Holy Mother, who are so good! May they bless Father Peter McCall, Maryanne Lacy and the wonderful people who do his work.

> Thank you dear Jesus for
> your divine blessing.
> Lucy Meo
> Bronxville, NY

Praise God from Whom All Blessings Flow

August 19, 1988
Dear Father McCall,

Three years ago I was diagnosed as having non-Hodgkin's lymphoma (cancer of the lymph glands) and I was started on a program of chemotherapy. The doctors who attended to me assured me that this type of treatment would put the cancer into remission. After sixteen months of chemo treatment however the doctors told me that they had exhausted all possible chemotherapy treatment and I was told that a different course of action must be taken.

A bone marrow transplant treatment was begun and took about 4-1/2 months to complete and once again I was given the bad news that this too was unsuccessful. The last option of radiation was offered, which I took. Treatments were started in October 1987 and were finished on January 1988. Treatments were once again unsuccessful. For the three years of treatment I attended your healing masses having been told of them by Elda Zamparo, a person from the prayer group from my Parish, St. Paul's in Congers, NY. Each time I went I felt peace within me that I had not know before. One night you told us how God was our Father and we His children, and if we asked our Father for help He would give it to us.I laid in bed that night and asked God for help and if it was His will that I would be healed.

In February of 1988 I started to hemorrhage internally. All the radiation treatments had burned my stomach and upper intestines. The doctors were unable to stop the bleeding and a surgeon was called in. The decision was made to remove a large portion of my stomach and intestines. I was prepared for surgery and given the anesthetic. The impending surgery at best would have left me severely disabled for the rest of my life. Louis Gerencaer and his wife, both members of St. Paul's prayer team were in the hospital and met my husband Ben, he told them of my being in surgery.

Mr. and Mrs. Gerencser, Ben and two close friends joined hands in a circle and prayed for me. While they prayed the surgeon changed his mind and decided surgery would not be done. They would try to allow the body to heal itself. When I came out of the recovery room, my husband told me how they had prayed for me. I knew then that God had answered our prayers. Fourteen days later the bleeding had stopped and I was sent home to recuperate.

In March 1988 I had a CAT scan that showed no change in the cancer, and the news that all cancer patients fear the most was given to me: "There will be no more treatments of any kind." The severe radiation burns to my stomach and intestines would not allow any more chemotherapy or radiation for fear of starting the hemorrhage again. Periodic CAT scans would be done to watch the tumors and that was all they could do.

A few nights later I went once again to your Healing Mass as we had done during this entire period. This night you laid your gentle hands upon me and I knew that I would get through this difficult time okay. It was as if God Himself said so.

On July 23, 1988 I had another CAT scan to check the tumors. My doctor's appointment was July 27, at that time he would tell me what the findings of the CAT scan were. I was sitting on the examination table when he entered the room. He sat on a chair facing me, "Dorothy, I read your CAT scan and the radiologist also read it. I don't know why, since you have had no chemo since last year and no radiation since January, but your tumors have all shrunk." He shook his head and said, "There is no accounting for it, none at all."

Praise God, I knew why. I can't even begin to explain the joy that filled my heart. I now know what you were telling me at your Healing Masses. I had asked my heavenly Father, and He had healed me. God bless you.

Dorothy Albertson
Valley Cottage, NY

This Is Holy Ground

March, 1991
Dear Father Peter and Maryanne,

Finally my thoughts of testimony on healing are now yours. In November 1989, at a Healing Mass, Maryanne called on someone needing a healing of an ovarian cyst on the right side. I sat and waited for someone to raise their hand. She called out several times in what seemed like forever, but in actuality about two minutes. I looked around and decided to raise my hand and go forward. Healing Masses were relatively new to me and I was so attentive to what was going to happen to me and around me that I couldn't concentrate on my prayers to God. I guess you could say that I didn't' "Let go, let God." Well, prayers and songs began and I felt myself falling back to the floor. I tried to pray, but couldn't. I tried to relax and I couldn't. Then I felt Maryanne's hand and a vibration and heat over my abdomen where she and Fr. Peter prayed for healing of the cysts and fibroid tumor. After I stayed a while, others came and prayed with me. I couldn't believe I was here and this was happening. It left me feeling "free" and "light", but also questioning a lot.

Previously, my first healing service was in May 1989. I wasn't sure what to expect; fanatics jumping, rehearsed fallings, healings, people swaying and praying. My sister, who went to one in New York City by Fr. Kelleher, told me to go with friends and just sit with my eyes closed and meditate. That's what I did. I never felt Jesus — His Spirit — more alive and present in a church than I did that night. It was so nice to see people coming to praise God because they wanted to instead of the usual Sunday crowd that goes just for going. Everyone was together here with a oneness so beautiful. I was also surprised to see so many from our Parish there too.

Services began with beautiful music and song from Bob and Marie. I sat, stood, knelt with eyes closed; sometimes a peek at who was here and there. It was during my own moments of meditation that I could hear what God was saying. I was then able to enjoy and feel a part of what was going on around me. I was able to give praise from my heart and mind instead of just following along with my lips. Today I thank God for his healing and blessings for me and others.

I began feeling a little guilty when I could not appreciate the actual day of calling and healing. But I realize now it was my first step. God opened the door not just for a physical healing, but an emotional and spiritual healing too! It took the months after and each time I attended healing services — for me to climb His stairway, to really understand and appreciate what my healing was all about. I was thankful but not 100% convinced that I had been physically healed. You see, doctors were still running tests and I was still hurting at times. Friends prayed for me and with me at times.

Then the morning of my surgery came — exploratory, laporscopy and partial or total hysterectomy. I was fine, but at the same time, nervous. I was totally unsure of what was going on. A friend, Peggy Broughal, came early that morning to take my kids Danielle and Mike to camp. In the two minutes she came and left she quickly

said, "Don't be afraid, Jesus is in you —
he will take any pain and you'll be fine —
and remember, you are healed, nothing
will be there." Well, I smiled, said "thanks
and goodbye." It wasn't until we pulled up
to the hospital that I shared what she said
with my husband, who was on his own
questioning quest about who God is.

Well, I was blessed when I found out
my friend was my nurse for the day, and
also a friend from long ago as my anes-
thesiologist. Surgery began and then I
woke up afterwards. My Doctor was there
as he promised. I asked how much of a
hysterectomy was done and if I had cancer? He said, "Nothing. It's okay." I said,
"What?" He said, "There was nothing, absolutely nothing, everything was perfect."
I said "The power of prayer." He smiled,
but didn't understand. He later told me all
my pain must have been in my head, that
it had been imagined. Then I asked how
about all the tests and sonograms for the
last three-one-half years, where we measured the sizes of cysts and tumor. And
where did they go? I knew the answer; he
couldn't give me any answer except a
shrug of the shoulders and "I don't know."
Healing is a wonderful fact of our lives
and a wonderful gift from God. We must
let Him heal all of us, not just parts of us.
And we must learn to be open with Him
and work with Him.

When I was asked to give testimony, it was hard for me at that time. God was still answering a lot of my questions. So when I spoke to the community gathered that night, I did not want to misrepresent God or the miracle He worked. I don't want people to think its magic or phoney, staged set-ups. I want people to believe some of God's healing happens 1,2,3, as Lazarus, or the little girl lying dead in bed; or sometimes because we're all 'individual'. God knows just the right way to handle each case. And I had mine, it wasn't just a snap of a finger, but a series of months, days and nights and it's still continuing in a growth in faith and understanding of God and also trust that He healed me. Thank you, Jesus.

Kathy Fayol
Bloomingburg, NY

I Believe in Miracles,

October 26, 1989
Dear Maryanne,

At your Saturday Healing Liturgy in December 1988 you prayed for me and I knew immediately the Lord touched me in a significant way. In November 1988, the night before my annual check-up, I discovered a lump under my arm. I visited several surgeons and all diagnosed it as a recurrence of malignant melanoma, the most severe and fastest moving type of skin cancer. This was shocking and flabbergasting to me and the physicians. The cancer I had in 1982 was considered so superficial that they said it could never recur. I had major surgery, a wide-excision of the spot, and a skin graft from my leg to my right arm, where the malignant freckle had been. This was considered the correct medical procedure for such a superficial malignancy.

I was scheduled for surgery at Sloan-Kettering Memorial for removal of the tumor on Monday, December 12, 1988. The CAT scan, taken soon before I went to the Healing Mass, showed the tumor in the auxilla (underarm, or place where the melanoma had recurred in the lymph system); it also showed spots on my lungs. The doctor was quite concerned about those spots, not knowing if they were cancer metastasis, old scar tissue, or current infection.

It was a very frightening time before the surgery. The doctors did not know how far the cancer had spread, or if it had metastasized. Our family had a horrible Thanksgiving — I had just been diagnosed — and our holiday was somber and sad, (even my nephew gave me a long, long hug and whispered, "Are you alright?") as we discussed what the doctors said about the possibilities of surgery, treatments, recurrence.

I felt like I had been shot, mortally wounded. I couldn't believe that this was happening — again. In fact the pathology lab from the first surgery wondered why I needed the original slides. When I told the head pathologist there apparently was a recurrence, he said, "That is statistically impossible." He continued, "I just looked at those slides again and the determination of the superficiality of the original malignancy was correct." I felt awful. Here, the treatment I had in 1982 was medically appropriate and six years later I had "statistically impossible" cancer. Day by day the lump became more annoying. At the Healing Mass, I was very uncomfortable since the lump was extremely irritating. Although I was fairly close to the front of the line, it seemed like there were lots of other people before me. You were praying on the right side of the altar and Father Peter on the left and a team about both of you. By the time I reached the front of the line you suddenly crossed the altar and changed positions. I was next and was sent to you. As soon as you touched me, I rested in the Spirit, but was able to talk with you. As you touched the lump under my arm, it felt as if you were pushing down on the spot with both hands and all your weight. But, you weren't, you were just touching the lump with one hand. I also felt like I was being shaken to pieces, the vibrations were so strong.

When you finished the prayer, I knew that the Lord had really touched me. Healed me. Healed the cancer. Though the lump remained, what was different was knowing that my fear was gone. My fear was that the cancer would recur or had metastasized further. I knew that it hadn't; that it wouldn't. I went into that operation unafraid.

It took sixteen days for the pathology reports to come back after the surgery, and yes, they were anxious days, especially for my mother and sister, as well as for me. The pathology report confirmed what I already knew in my spirit — only the one lymph node was malignant. None of the other 22 lymph nodes (from under my arm) was involved, although some were enlarged on the CAT scan. Fortunately, I did not require any additional treatments — neither radiation, chemotherapy, or immunotherapy. Along the way I've learned that God wants us to be well. He who loves us so much doesn't make us sick, although He allows it and can work through it. I know also that He never promised us a rose garden, but has promised us the victory. And sometimes, you know that you know the victory. I know this cancer is gone and will not recur. Nothing can change that conviction. I believe the pathology reports confirmed that and something else as well. Something truly miraculous. In May 1989, I had a second CAT scan — the first since before the surgery and your prayers. The CAT scan showed no spots on my lungs!

I have regular chest X-rays and blood tests. The doctor didn't have any explanation for spots on my lungs or what they could have been. No, there couldn't be a mistake on the first film. Hallelujah! I believe in miracles. Whatever it was — cancer, scar, infection or other — it is no longer there. I believe that is the miraculous proof that my healing from cancer is complete. Thank you for praying with me and for being the Lord's instrument of healing for me. I don't think it was an accident that suddenly you crossed the altar and I went to you for prayer. I hope Jesus continues to use you in such mighty ways, and thank you for your openness to the Lord.

Barbara O'Reilly
New York, NY

Epilogue

THE PRAYER THAT HEALS

We have become, over the years, very much aware that there is no one particular prayer that heals. A prayer that was effective with one person may not be effective with another person. In fact, we know that the words we say are not as important as the inner content of our attitudes, motivations, and beliefs. Whenever we are tempted to write down certain guidelines about how to pray for healing, we must remember the miracle story in John's Gospel (5:1-17) where Jesus heals a lame man who not only does not make an act of faith in Jesus, but who doesn't even know Jesus' name. It's stories such as this that tell us that there is always a mystery around healing prayer and we should not be so arrogant as to presume we know all the answers. Having said this, we will now outline a prayer technique which we have found to be very effective.

Effective healing prayer is not found in magical words, secret gestures, or exotic postures. Nor can we say that effective healing prayer is found in special attitudes, dispositions, or levels of consciousness, which once attained, would guarantee healing. We can never manipulate divine healing by saying certain words or doing certain gestures that force God to comply with our demands. We must realize that we do not always know what is for another's highest good, so we must leave all conclusions up to God.

The overwhelming message of healing is found in the repeated words of Jesus, "Your faith has made you whole" (Mt 9:22) or, "Let it be done to you according to your faith" (Mt 9:29). We are told in the Letter of James (5:15), that "the prayer of faith will heal the sick person". We constantly see Jesus in the Gospels, either affirming a person's faith or eliciting a person's faith before healing. Faith, then, is the key ingredient to effective healing prayer. We know that a little bit of practical faith is more powerful than a lot of theoretical faith. In other words, it is more effective to believe that God can and will heal in a particular situation than to believe that God can heal in general.

Our experience has taught us the power of shared affirmative prayer. Praying alone can be effective, but we have discovered the power of united prayer where two or three come together in the Name of Jesus and simply agree that God is, in fact, hearing and answering the prayers of the group. We have put together what we call "Guidelines for a Creative Prayer Group." We have used this prayer form very effectively on our retreats and days of recollection. Some of the members of our ministry use this prayer form when they meet together for weekly prayer.

We believe that what makes this prayer form so powerful is the joining of at least two people to "agree in the Name of Jesus" that God is in fact answering their prayers. Jesus told us, "Amen, I say to you, if two of you agree on earth about anything for which they are to pray, it shall be granted to them by my Heavenly Father. For where two or three are gathered in my Name, there am I in the midst of them" (Mt 18:19-20).

Another reason why this prayer form is so effective is that the partners are not to give advice to one another, but to allow the Holy Spirit to answer the prayer directly. Too often our own prejudices and opinions only interfere with the Holy Spirit's answer to our prayers. The only function of the prayer partners is to practice the presence of God and to assure one another that their prayers are being answered. The Holy Spirit must be allowed to have complete control of the outcome of the prayer requests which will be given directly to the person praying and must not come from one of the partners.

We invite you to try this form of healing prayer. We invite you to let go of any preconceived ideas you may have about healing prayer and simply join with another to make conscious contact with the Holy Spirit, and watch the Holy Spirit answer your prayers.

Guidelines for a Creative Prayer Group

The purpose of a Creative Prayer Group is to join together to establish conscious contact with the Holy Spirit and for the members of the group to experience a greater awareness of the power of the Holy Spirit working in and through them. The goal is not to solve the problems of the members by the members, but to turn all problems, needs for healing, and prayer requests over to the Holy Spirit.

The ideal size of the group is between two and five members. Meetings can take place on a daily basis or just once a week. Meetings should be brief and to the point.

The meeting begins with united prayer and praise recalling to mind the presence and power of the Holy Spirit. The partners try to the best of their ability to remove any blocks to the awareness of God's presence. In other words, each partner practices the Presence of God in a manner which is most conducive to the individual. One partner acts as leader and reminds the group that the Presence of God is with them and waiting to respond to them in a very loving and personal way as they join to pray.

The leader takes the group through the steps one at a time. Each member repeats the steps in the exact or similar words. All do Step #1 at the same time as well as the rest of the Steps. When Step #5 is reached, each member takes turns expressing his or her prayer requests. The other members of the group give that person their complete attention. This is called "unconditional positive regard." No advice or counsel is to be given. The other members simply affirm the power of the Holy Spirit to help and heal. They can use an affirmation similar to: "I know that the Holy Spirit has heard your prayer and that you will experience what you ask for or something better."

It is extremely important that the members do not interfere with the working of the Holy Spirit by offering their own solutions to the problems expressed. No matter how "inspired" another member may feel about giving a suggestion, they are to refrain from doing so because the Holy Spirit will answer the person directly by way of intuitions and reassurances. The group simply prays with the person as the Holy Spirit leads them. After the prayers, the person recites Step #6.

When each person has been prayed with, the prayer session ends with everyone reciting Step #7 together.

Seven Steps to a Creative Prayer Session

Step #1 Surrendering

"I admit that I am personally powerless to improve life. I need help."

Step #2 Believing

"I believe in the power and the presence of the Holy Spirit to whom all things are possible. I believe that this power is available to me and wants to help me."

Step #3 Deciding

"I make a decision to place myself completely under the influence and direction of the Holy Spirit. I ask the Holy Spirit to take complete charge of my life and change me lovingly and gently at the root of my being."

Step #4 Releasing

"To establish my conscious contact with the Holy Spirit, I get honest with myself as never before and willingly release all negative judgment and emotions that I have directed at myself and others. I am willing to forgive all hurts as the Holy Spirit leads me."

Step #5 Asking

"I speak directly to the group and to the Holy Spirit about any healing need, problem, or special project important to me, asking for help, healing and guidance from the Holy Spirit." (Here each person mentions their prayer requests. The others give them their undivided attention and assures the person of a good outcome to their prayers. No advice or solutions are given).

Step #6 Thanksgiving

"I give thanks that the Holy Spirit has responded to my every need and that my life has dramatically changed."

Step #7 Dedication and Agreement

"I now have an agreement with the Holy Spirit and I go out into my life with a spirit of enthusiasm, Excitement, and expectancy. The Holy Spirit will supply me with an abundance of all things necessary to fulfill my needs. I am at peace."

The prayer session ends with this final step. It is good not to talk about what went on during the session because of the possibility of members bringing up their own solutions to problems. What we consider helpful may not be the direction toward which the Holy Spirit is leading that person.

ABOUT THE AUTHORS

Father Peter McCall, OFM Cap.

Father Peter, a Capuchin-Franciscan, was ordained a priest in 1962. He taught high school religion for seventeen years, ten years of which were on Guam in the Marianas Islands and seven years at Sacred Heart High School, Yonkers, New York. He was the leader of the Sacred Heart Prayer Group in Yonkers from 1978-1982. He then was reassigned from his teaching duties at Sacred Heart in 1981 and given permission to work full-time in the healing ministry. Father Peter has been a member of the Association of Christian Therapists since 1979. Father Peter has a Masters Degree from Fordham University in Educational Psychology, plus graduate studies in Scripture and Spirituality at Fordham. He has attended the Catholic Charismatic Biblical Institute at St. Mary's University, San Antonio, Texas.

Father Peter is the author of many pamphlets relating to the issues of dysfunctional family systems and is also the co-author of *An Invitation to Healing*. He is the author of many audio cassette teachings on healing prayer.

Maryanne Lacy

Maryanne is the mother of five children and lives in Hastings-on-Hudson, New York. She graduated in 1982 from the training program in Spiritual

Development and Peer Guidance and in 1983 from the program in Spiritual Direction and Religious Counseling. Both programs are sponsored by the New York Archdiocese Center for Spiritual Development. She also has had further training in Spiritual Development and the Spiritual Exercises of St. Ignatius. Maryanne has been a member of the Association of Christian Therapists since 1979. She was leader of the St. Matthew's prayer group in Hastings-on-Hudson, New York from 1978-1982. Maryanne first manifested the gift of healing in 1976 when she was praying over a woman who had a growth in her throat. The woman was healed instantly.

Maryanne has co-authored, with Father Peter, the book *An Invitation to Healing.* She is also the author of many meditation tapes relating to healing prayer. Together they founded a healing prayer center in 1981, which is called The House of Peace located in its present headquarters in the Bronx, NY.

Both Father Peter and Maryanne Lacy have done extensive healing work through retreats, days of recollection and workshops. They have conducted Healing Masses and services all over the USA and in Ireland. They have been the keynote speakers at many Charismatic conferences. They continue to update themselves on the current issues related to the twelve step programs and holistic healing.

BOOKS AND TAPES AVAILABLE

Please order from:
House of Peace
PO Box 696
1291 Allerton Avenue
Bronx, NY 10469 (212) 547-3230

Please include NY State Tax if applicable,
and shipping charge as follows:
Orders under $7.00, add $1.50
Orders under $25.00, add $3.00
Orders over $25.00, add 7%
Please make checks payable to:
House of Peace

Tapes by Father Peter McCall

#101 THE GOOD NEWS OF HEALING An eight audio cassette album containing thirty-two selected homilies by Father Peter from the First Saturday Healing Masses at Blessed Sacrament Monastery Chapel. $35.00

#102 HEALING WISDOM Six teachings on the power of wisdom to heal. Given during the first six months of 1991 at the First Saturday Masses. $24.00

#103 CHARISMATIC TWELVE STEP SPIRITUALITY A talk given by Father Peter at the New York Regional Conference of the Association of Christian Therapists, 1988. $7.00

#104 THE WISDOM OF JESUS Six teachings on the wisdom of Jesus that heals. They were given during the second six months of 1991 at the First Saturday Masses. $24.00

Tapes by Maryanne Lacy

#201 THE HEALING TRUTH WILL SET YOU FREE. A soothing and reconciling meditation aimed at our perception of God the father. $9.00

#202 THE MIRACLE OF WHO YOU ARE. An inspiring meditation based on Psalm 139 leading to healing for various parts of the body. $9.00

#203 HEALING: PRACTICING THE PRESENCE OF GOD. A stimulating meditation to help the listener realize and claim the presence of the holiness of God within each one of us · $9.00

#204 HEALING THROUGH THE GIFT OF TONGUES. An anointed prayer which Maryanne sings in the gift of tongues with her graceful voice to invoke healing. $9.00

#205 PRAYERS FROM AN INVITATION TO HEALING A beautiful tape by Maryanne Lacy and Richard Licata based on the popular prayers in the book, An Invitation to Healing. One of the prayers is the well-known Prayer for Continuous Healing. $10.00

BOOK:

AN INVITATION TO HEALING, House of Peace, 1985. Now in its second printing, this book by Fr. Peter & Maryanne is considered by many the best "primer" on the healing ministry. $9.95

PAMPHLETS:

Cost is 25c each or 10c each for orders over fifty.

P#1 A VISION TO CHANGE A VISION
The story of the House of Peace

P#2 WHEN IS SUFFERING GOOD FOR YOU?

P#3 AN INVITATION TO ABUNDANT LIFE

P#4 WHAT IS GENERATIONAL HEALING?

P#5 THERE IS VICTORY OVER CANCER*

P#6 THE HEALING OF CO-DEPENDENCE*

Rise and Be Healed

P#7 THE EIGHT BEATITUDES OF FORGIVING LIVING

P#8 THE PRAYER FOR CONTINUOUS HEALING

P#9 PRAYER IN TIME OF DISTRESS

P#10 HEALING THROUGH MEDITATION

P#11 HEALING OUR SHAME*

P#12 SEVEN SEEDS OF DISEASE & HEALING

P#13 WHAT IS SPIRITUAL HEALING?

P#14 TWELVE STEPS TO HEALING & LIBERATION

P#15 WHAT IS THE DIFFERENCE BETWEEN RELIGION & SPIRITUALITY?

P#16 THE HEALING OF ADULT CHILDREN

P#17 HEALING PRAYER AND CO-DEPENDENT ISSUES

P#18 FROM VICTIM TO VICTOR

P#19 RELIGIOUS ADDICTION & ABUSE*

P#20 THE PRAYER THAT HEALS

* Dove Pamphlets from Pecos, NM